Sixth

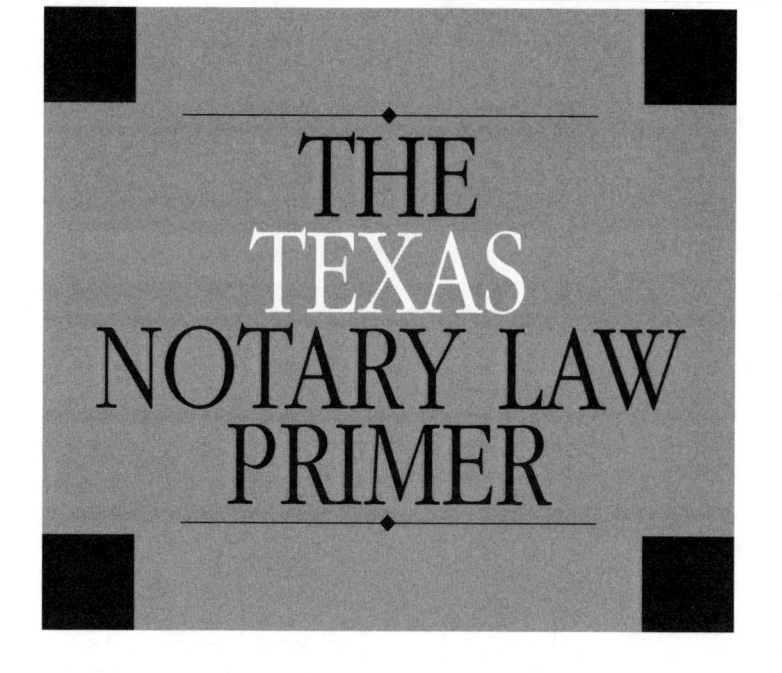

THE TEXAS NOTARY LAW PRIMER

All the hard-to-find information every Texas Notary Public needs to know!

National Notary Association

Published by:

National Notary Association
9350 De Soto Ave., P.O. Box 2402
Chatsworth, CA 91313-2402
Telephone: 1-818-739-4000
FAX: 1-818-700-0920
E-mail: nna@nationalnotary.org
Web site: www.nationalnotary.org

Copyright © 1998 National Notary Association
ALL RIGHTS RESERVED. No part of this book may be reproduced in any form without permission in writing from the publisher.

This information is provided to aid comprehension of state Notary Public requirements and should not be construed as legal advice. Please consult an attorney for inquiries relating to legal matters.

Sixth Edition
First Edition © 1980

ISSN No. 1097-5462
ISBN No. 1-891133-03-9

Table of Contents

Introduction 1

How to Become a Texas Notary Public 3

Tools of the Trade 5

10 Most-Asked Questions 7

Steps to Proper Notarization 12

Notary Laws Explained 17
    The Notary Commission 17
    Official Notarial Acts 21
    Practices and Procedures 40
    Misconduct, Fines and Penalties 60

Test Your Knowledge 65

Texas Laws Pertaining to Notaries Public 71

Office of the Texas Secretary of State 99

County Clerks' Offices 100

Bureaus of Vital Statistics 108

Hague Convention Nations 113

About the Publisher 116

Index 118

Introduction

You are to be commended on your interest in Texas Notary law! Purchasing *The Texas Notary Law Primer* identifies you as a conscientious professional who takes your official responsibilities seriously.

In few fields is the expression "more to it than meets the eye" truer than in Notary law. What often appears on the surface to be a simple procedure may, in fact, have important legal considerations.

The purpose of *The Texas Notary Law Primer* is to provide you with a resource to help decipher the many intricate laws that affect notarization. In doing so, the *Primer* will acquaint you with all important aspects of Texas Notary law and with prudent notarial practices in general.

This 1998 edition is the most recent and most exhaustive revision of *The Texas Notary Law Primer* — a text that has been continuously revised and updated since its initial publication in 1980. Of course, this edition has been completely updated with the many recent law changes. The most notable of these changes include provisions that allow a Notary to sign a document for a person who is physically unable to sign.

While *The Texas Notary Law Primer* begins with informative chapters on how to obtain your commission, what tools the Notary needs, often-asked questions, and critical steps in notarization, the heart of this book is the chapter entitled "Notary Laws Explained." Here, we take you through the myriad of Notary laws and put them in easy-to-understand terms. Every pertinent section of the law is analyzed and explained, as well as topics not covered by Texas law but nonetheless of vital concern to you as a Notary.

For handy reference, we have reprinted the complete text of the laws of Texas that relate to the duties of Notaries Public. In addition, we have included addresses and phone numbers of the Secretary of State's office, Texas County Clerk offices and Bureaus of Vital Statistics, plus a list of nations that are parties to the Hague Convention, a treaty which simplifies the process of authentication.

Whether you're about to be commissioned for the first time, or a longtime Notary, we're sure *The Texas Notary Law Primer* will provide you with new insights and understanding. Your improved comprehension of Texas Notary law will naturally result in greater competence as a professional Notary Public.

                              Milton G. Valera
                              President
                              National Notary Association

How to Become a Texas Notary Public

1. Ensure that you comply with the basic qualifications for a Texas Notary commission.

First, you must be a legal resident of the state. Second, you must be 18 years of age or older. And third, you must not have been convicted of a felony or any crime involving moral turpitude.

U.S. citizenship is not required as long as you legally reside in this country under federal law. There is no minimum time of state residency — you can apply for a commission on the same day you enter Texas.

2. Obtain a commission application form.

The official application for a Texas Notary commission is available from the Secretary of State by calling 1-512-463-5705. You may also obtain an application in person or through the mail at the addresses below. If you are renewing your current Notary commission, request an application for reappointment from the same office. The renewal application will not automatically be sent upon expiration.

Street Address:
Secretary of State
Notary Public Unit
1019 Brazos, #214
Austin, TX 78701

Mailing Address:
Secretary of State
Notary Public Unit
P.O. Box 12079
Austin, TX 78711-2079

3. Complete the application form.

Fill out the application, typing or printing neatly in ink. Be aware that any misstatement or omission of requested information is cause for denial or later revocation of a Notary commission.

4. Purchase your Notary bond.

The Notary application will include a surety bond form. Take or mail this form to a licensed surety company and purchase a $10,000 Notary bond.

5. Submit the application with the commission fees and your Notary bond.

The completed and signed application must be mailed or delivered to the Secretary of State's Notary Public Unit at the address on page 3. A $21 fee — payable to "Secretary of State" — and the surety bond must be enclosed with the application.

If you are renewing your Notary appointment, the application must be submitted no earlier than 90 days before your current appointment expires. However, if the application is submitted *past* the expiration date, there will be *no grace period* allowing you to notarize during the gap between appointments.

6. Take and sign your oath of office.

Once your application has been approved, the Secretary of State will send you your official Notary commission. On the commission is the official oath of office, which must be signed and executed before an officer authorized to administer oaths — a Notary Public, for example, but *not* yourself. Although you must take an oath of office, the oath itself is not required to be filed with the Secretary of State.

7. Obtain an official Notary seal and journal.

Before you perform any notarial act with your new Notary commission, you must obtain an official seal of office and an official journal of notarial acts. See "Notary Seal" on pages 48–49 for the specific requirements of Texas law regarding a Notary seal.

In addition, you must also obtain or make a schedule of the maximum fees that Texas statute allows Notaries to charge. This schedule must be posted in a conspicuous place in the office where you will notarize. ■

Tools of the Trade

There are several tools that Notaries need to carry out their duties lawfully and efficiently. These tools are as important to the Notary as a hammer and saw are to the carpenter.

Inking Seal

The inked rubber seal affixes a photographically reproducible impression in indelible ink. It is a convenient official seal for notarizing deeds and other documents that will be submitted to a public recorder for microfilming. The Notary's seal must include the words "Notary Public, State of Texas" around a star of five points, the Notary's name and the expiration date of the Notary's commission.

Seal Embosser

The embosser may be used by itself as an official Texas Notary seal; however, when an embosser is affixed on documents that will be publicly recorded and microfilmed (deeds, etc.), the resulting impression *must* be smudged with ink, graphite or carbon to become photographically reproducible. Many Notaries use an embosser as a fraud deterrent in addition to an inking seal; embossing pages and certificates together deters their fraudulent replacement. Because photocopies of documents can easily pass as originals today, the embossment can be used to distinguish an original from a photocopy. When used in conjunction with an inking seal, the embossment does not have to be smudged.

Journal of Notarial Acts

The Notary is required by law to keep a journal record of

every document notarized. The journal record must include the date of the document, the date of the notarization, the name and residence of the parties whose signatures are being notarized, the type of information used to verify the identity of the signers, and a brief description of the document. The Notary's journal provides a record of notarial transactions that may be used as evidence in a court proceeding.

Jurat Stamp

The jurat stamp impresses on an affidavit the jurat wording "Subscribed and sworn to before me this _____ day of _____, _____ by _____." The jurat stamp is more convenient (and safer, since critical wording will not be omitted) than typing the wording on each affidavit that requires it.

Venue Stamp

The venue stamp is used in conjunction with the jurat stamp in a jurat. The phrase, "State of _____, County of _____," indicates where the jurat was executed. Also usable for acknowledgments.

Fingerprinting Device

Though not required by law, asking a signer to leave a thumbprint in the Notary's journal is a strong deterrent to forgers. Small, inexpensive devices make taking a print easy.

Notarial Certificates

Preprinted notarial certificates for acknowledgments, jurats, proofs of execution by subscribing witness, and for copy certification by document custodian are available.

Errors and Omissions Insurance

Notary errors and omissions insurance provides protection for Notaries who are sued for damages resulting from unintentional notarial mistakes. In the event of a lawsuit, the "E&O" insurance company will provide and pay for the Notary's legal counsel and absorb any damages levied by a court or agreed to in a settlement, up to the policy coverage limit. Errors and omissions insurance does not cover the Notary for intentional misconduct. ■

As a full-service organization, the National Notary Association makes available to Texas Notaries all notarial items required by law, custom and convenience.

10 Most-Asked Questions

Every Notary has a question or two about whether and how to notarize. But there are certain questions that pop up again and again. These top 10 are asked repeatedly at the National Notary Association's seminars, its annual National Conference of Notaries Public and through its *Notary Information Service*.

As with most questions about notarization, the answer to these 10 is not always a simple "yes" or "no." Rather, the answer is, "It depends...."

Here's what every Notary wants to know:

1. Can I notarize a will?

Sometimes. A Notary should only notarize a document described as a will if clear instructions and a notarial certificate are provided. If the signer of the will is relying on the Notary for advice on how to proceed, the Notary should tell the individual to see an attorney.

Laws regarding wills differ from state to state. Some states do not require notarization of wills, while others allow it as one of several witnessing options. Often it is not the will itself that is notarized, but accompanying affidavits signed by witnesses.

The danger in notarizing wills is that would-be testators who have drafted their own wills without legal advice may believe that notarization will make their wills legal and valid. However, even when notarized, such homemade wills may be worthless because the testators failed to obtain the proper number of witnesses or omitted important information.

In fact, notarization itself may actually void an otherwise properly executed handwritten (holographic) will, because courts have occasionally held that any writing on the document other than the testator's invalidates the will.

2. Can I notarize for a stranger with no identification?

Yes. If identification of a signer cannot be based on personal knowledge or identification documents (ID cards), a Notary may rely on the oath or affirmation of one personally known credible identifying witness to identify an unknown signer.

The Notary must personally know the credible identifying witness, who must personally know the document signer. This establishes a chain of personal knowledge from the Notary to the credible identifying witness to the signer.

A credible identifying witness should be someone the Notary believes to be trustworthy and impartial. If a person has a financial or other beneficial interest in a document, that individual could not be a reliable witness.

When no credible identifying witness is available to identify a stranger without IDs, the Notary may have no choice but to tell the signer to find a personally known Notary or a friend who personally knows a Notary, if the signer is unable to obtain an adequate identification document.

3. Can I notarize a photograph?

No. To simply stamp and sign a photograph is improper. A Notary's signature and seal must appear only on a notarial certificate (such as an acknowledgment or jurat) accompanying a written statement signed by another person.

However, a signature on a written statement referring to an accompanying or attached photograph may be notarized; if the photograph is large enough, the statement and notarial certificate might even appear on its reverse side. Such a format may be acceptable when notarized photos are requested by persons seeking medical or health licenses, or by legal resident aliens renewing foreign passports.

A word of caution here: a Notary should always be suspicious about notarizing a photo-bearing card or document that could be used as a bogus "official" ID.

4. What if there's no room for my seal or if it smears?

Usually, if notarial wording printed on a document leaves no room for a seal, a loose certificate can be attached and filled out instead, if the certificate wording is substantially the same as on the document.

If an initial seal impression is unreadable and there is ample room on the document, another impression can be affixed nearby. The illegibility of the first impression will indicate why a second seal impression was necessary. The Notary should record in the journal that a second seal was applied.

A Notary should *never* attempt to fix an imperfect seal impression with pen, ink or correction fluid. This may be viewed as evidence of tampering and cause the document's rejection by a recorder.

5. Can I notarize signatures on photocopies of documents?

Yes. A photocopy may be notarized as long as it bears an *original* signature. That is, the photocopy must have been signed with pen and ink. A photocopied signature may *never* be notarized.

Note that some public recorders will not accept notarized signatures on photocopied sheets because the document will not adequately reproduce in microfilming.

When carbon copies are made, the Notary will sometimes be asked to conform rather than to notarize the copies. To conform a copy, the Notary reaffixes the official seal on the copy (carbon will not readily transfer a seal impression) and writes "conformed copy" prominently across the copy.

6. May I notarize for customers only?

No. As a public official, a Notary is not commissioned to serve just the customers or clients of any one business, even when the Notary's employer has paid for the bond, commissioning fees and notarial supplies. There is no such officer as a "Notary Private."

It is ethically improper — although hardly ever explicitly prohibited by statute — to discriminate between customers and noncustomers in offering or refusing to offer notarial services and in charging or not charging fees.

Discrimination against anyone who presents a lawful request for notarization is not a suitable policy for a public official commissioned to serve all of the public equally. Also, such discrimination can provide the basis for lawsuits.

7. Can I notarize a document in a language I can't read?

Perhaps. As long as the notarial certificate and document signature are in a language the Notary *can* read, Texas Notaries are not expressly prohibited from notarizing a document written in a language they *cannot* read.

However, there are certain difficulties and dangers in doing so. The main difficulty for the Notary is making an accurate journal description of an unreadable document; the main danger is that the document may be blatantly fraudulent. It is always preferable to refer such documents to a bilingual Notary who can read the language.

Under no circumstances should a notarization be performed if the Notary and the principal signer cannot communicate in the same language.

8. Can I certify a copy of a birth certificate?

No. While Texas Notaries are authorized to certify copies, they are specifically prohibited from certifying copies of documents that are either public records or publicly recordable.

Only an officer in a bureau of vital statistics should certify a copy of a birth certificate or other vital public record; a Notary's "certification" of a birth or death record may actually lend credibility to a counterfeit or tampered document. Only a county recording official should certify a copy of a deed or other recordable instrument.

The types of documents that Texas Notaries may properly certify copies of are original personal papers such as college diplomas, letters and in-house business documents.

9. Does a document have to be signed in my presence?

No and yes. Documents requiring acknowledgments normally do not need to be signed in the Notary's presence. However, the signer *must* appear before the Notary at the time of notarization to acknowledge that he or she freely signed for the purposes stated in the document.

An acknowledgment certificate indicates that the signer personally appeared before the Notary, was identified by the Notary, and acknowledged to the Notary that the document was freely signed.

On the other hand, documents requiring a jurat *must* indeed be signed in the Notary's presence, as dictated by the typical jurat wording, "Subscribed (signed) and sworn to before me...."

In executing a jurat, a Notary guarantees that the signer personally appeared before the Notary, was given an oath or affirmation by the Notary, and signed in the Notary's presence. In addition, even though it may not be a statutory requirement that the Notary positively identify a signer for a jurat, it is always a good idea to do so.

10. Can I notarize for a family member?

Yes and no. Although state law does not directly address notarizing for family members, the Secretary of State advises that a Notary should not notarize in these cases. Notaries who do so may violate the statutes prohibiting a direct beneficial interest — especially in notarizing for spouses in states, like Texas, with community property laws.

Besides the possibility of a financial interest in notarizing for a relative, there may be an "emotional interest" that can prevent the Notary from acting impartially. For example, a Notary who is asked to notarize a contract signed by his brother might attempt to persuade the sibling to sign or not sign. As a brother, the individual is entitled to exert influence — but this is entirely improper for a Notary.

Even if a Notary has no direct beneficial interest in the document and does not attempt to influence the signer, notarizing for a relative could subject the document to a legal challenge if other parties to the transaction allege that the Notary could not have acted impartially. ■

Steps to Proper Notarization

What constitutes reasonable care?

If a Notary can convincingly show that he or she used every reasonable precaution expected of a person of ordinary prudence and intelligence, then the Notary has exercised reasonable care — a shield against liability.

While it would be impossible to compile an all-inclusive list of the actions constituting reasonable care in every possible case, the following 14-step checklist will help Notaries avoid the most common pitfalls.

1. Require every signer to personally appear.

The signer *must* appear in person before the Notary on the date and in the county stated in the notarial certificate. "Personal appearance" means the signer is in the Notary's physical presence — face to face in the same room. A telephone call is not acceptable in lieu of personal appearance.

2. Make a careful identification.

The Notary should identify every document signer through either personal knowledge, the oath of a credible identifying witness, or through reliable identification documents (ID cards).

When using ID cards, the Notary must examine them closely to detect alteration, counterfeiting or evidence that they are issued to an impostor. Don't rely on a type of card with which you are unfamiliar, unless you check it against a reference such as the *U.S. Identification Manual* or the *ID Checking Guide*.

3. Feel certain the signer is competent.

A conscientious and careful Notary will be certain not only of the signer's identity and willingness to sign, but also will make a layperson's judgment about the signer's ability to understand the document. This ability to understand is called competence.

While Texas law does not expressly require the Notary to make a judgment about competence, it is in the Notary's best interest to do so. A document signer who is not able to respond intelligibly in a simple conversation with the Notary should not be considered competent to sign at that moment.

If in doubt, the Notary can ask the signer if he or she understands the document and can explain its purpose. Or, if the notarization is to be performed in a medical environment while the signer is under medical care, the signer's doctor can be consulted for a professional opinion.

4. Check the signature.

The Notary must make sure that the document signer signs the same name appearing on the identification presented.

To check for possible forgery, the Notary should compare the signature that the person leaves in the journal of notarial acts against the signatures on the document and on the IDs. Also, it should be noted whether the signer appears to be laboring on the journal signature, a possible indication of forgery in progress. (While Texas law does not require the document signer to also sign in the Notary's journal, prudent Notaries will always ask for a journal signature.)

In certain circumstances, it may be acceptable to make allowances for a signer who is signing with an abbreviated form of his name (John D. Smith instead of John David Smith), as long as the individual is signing with *less* than and not *more* than what is on the identification document.

5. Look for blank spaces.

Although not expressly prohibited by Texas law, notarization of incomplete documents is an unwise practice.

Documents with blank spaces have a great potential for fraudulent misuse. A borrower, for example, might sign an incomplete promissory note, trusting the lender to fill it out, and then later find that the lender has written in an amount in excess of what was actually borrowed.

If the blanks are inapplicable and intended to be left unfilled, the signer may be asked to line through each space (using ink), or to write in "not applicable" or "NA."

6. Scan the document.

Notaries are not required to read the documents they notarize. However, they should note certain important particulars about a document, such as its title, for recording in the journal of notarial acts. Notaries must be sure to count and record the number of pages; this can show whether pages are later fraudulently added or removed.

7. Check the document's date.

For acknowledgments, the date of signing on the document must either precede or be the same as the date of the notarization; it should not follow it. For a jurat, the document signing date and the notarization date must be the same.

A document dated to follow the date on its notarial certificate risks rejection by a recorder, who may question how the document could have been notarized before it was signed.

8. Keep a journal of notarial acts.

A journal is mandatory for all Notaries in Texas. If a notarized document is lost or altered, or if certain facts about the transaction are later challenged, the Notary's journal becomes valuable evidence. It can protect the rights of all parties to a transaction and help Notaries defend themselves against false accusations.

The Notary should include *all* the pertinent details of the notarization in the journal, such as the date and type of notarization, the date and type of document, the name and address of the signer, how this person was identified and notarial fees charged, if any. In addition, any other pertinent data, such as the representative capacity the signer is claiming, may be entered. Signers may also be asked to leave a signature and/or a thumbprint in the Notary's journal as a deterrent to fraud, though this is not required by law in Texas.

9. Complete the journal entry first.

The Notary should complete the journal entry entirely *before* filling out the notarial certificate. This prevents a signer from leaving before the important public record of the notarization is made in the journal.

10. Make sure the document has notarial wording.

If a notarial certificate does not come with the document, the Notary must ask the document signer what type of notarization

— acknowledgment, jurat or other — is required. The Notary may then type the appropriate notarial wording on the document or attach a preprinted, loose certificate.

If the signer does not know what type of notarization is required, he or she should contact the document's issuing or receiving agency to determine the type of notarization needed. This decision is *never* the Notary's to make unless the Notary is also an attorney.

11. Be attentive to details.

When filling out the certificate, the Notary needs to make sure the venue correctly identifies the place of notarization. If the venue is preprinted and incorrect, the Notary must line through the incorrect state and/or county, write in the proper site of the notarization, and initial and date the change.

Also, the Notary must pay attention to spaces on the notarial certificate that indicate the number and gender of the document signers, as well as how they were identified — for example, leave the plural "(s)" in "person(s)" untouched or cross it out, as appropriate.

12. Affix your signature and seal properly.

Notaries should sign *exactly* the same name appearing on their commissioning papers. And they must never forget to affix their official seals — a common reason for rejection of a document by a recorder.

The seal should be placed as close to the Notary's signature as possible without overprinting it. To prevent illegibility, a Notary seal should not be affixed over wording, particularly over a signature. Although an embossment may be placed over the letters "L.S.," an inked seal impression should be affixed next to but not over them to ensure legibility of data in the seal.

13. Protect loose certificates.

If the Notary has to attach a notarial certificate, it must be securely stapled to the left margin of the document. Notaries can protect against the removal of such loose certificates by embossing them together with the documents and writing the particulars of the document to which the certificate is attached in one of the certificate's margins. For example, the notation, "This certificate is attached to a 15-page partnership agreement between John Smith and Mary Doe, signed July 14, 1997," would deter fraudulent removal and reattachment of a loose certificate.

14. Don't give advice.

Every state prohibits nonattorneys from practicing law. Notaries should *never* prepare or complete documents for others, nor give advice on any matter relating to a document unless they are attorneys or professionals certified or licensed in a relevant area of expertise. The nonattorney Notary *never* chooses the type of certificate or notarization a document needs, since this decision can have important legal ramifications. The Notary could be held liable for any damages resulting from an incorrectly chosen certificate or notarization. ∎

Notary Laws Explained

In layperson's language, this chapter discusses and clarifies key parts of the laws of Texas that regulate Notaries Public. Most of these laws are reprinted in full in "Texas Laws Pertaining to Notaries Public," beginning on page 71.

This edition explains the significant changes to Texas law that allow a Notary to sign a document for a person who is unable to sign, as well as provisions that clarify the definition of "satisfactory evidence."

In the text that follows, these abbreviations are used:

TGC. Texas Government Code, which contains most of the laws regulating the activities of Notaries Public.

TCPRC. Texas Civil Practices and Remedies Code, which sets rules for the taking of acknowledgments and proofs of written instruments.

NPEM. *Notary Public Educational Materials*, issued to newly commissioned Notaries Public by the Secretary of State.

THE NOTARY COMMISSION

Application for Commission

Qualifications. To become a Notary in Texas, the applicant must: (TGC, Sec. 406.004)

1) Be at least 18 years old;

2) Be a legal resident of Texas; and

3) Not have been convicted of a felony or any crime involving moral turpitude.

In addition, the applicant must properly complete and submit the Notary application, obtain a $10,000 bond (see "Notary Bond," below), and pay all required fees (see Application Fee," following). Once commissioned, the Notary must also take and sign the oath of office (see "Oath of Office," page 19). (TGC, Sec. 406.006)

Application Fee. The total fee for a Notary commission applicant is $21. This includes $10 for approving and filing the bond, $10 for the commission itself, and $1 for the Secretary of State to employ an investigator and to prepare and distribute commissioning materials. (TGC, Sec. 406.007)

Rejection of Application. The Secretary of State may reject a Notary application for: (TGC, Sec. 406.009)

- A false statement knowingly made in the application;

- A conviction for a felony or a crime involving moral turpitude;

- An imposition of an administrative, criminal or civil penalty or a conviction for a violation of Notary law in Texas or another state;

- Failure to comply with Texas Government Code, Section 406.017, regarding false advertising, misrepresentation and illegal translation of the words "Notary Public" into Spanish; or

- Performing a notarization without requiring personal appearance of the signer.

Reappointment. A Notary may not apply to renew his or her commission earlier than 90 days before the expiration of the Notary's current commission. (TGC, Sec. 406.011)

Notary Bond

Requirement. Every Texas Notary is required to obtain a bond of $10,000 and file it with the Notary application at the office of the Secretary of State. (TGC, Sec. 406.010)

The Notary bond must be purchased from a surety company authorized to do business in the state. The bond must be approved by the Secretary of State, payable to the Governor, and conditioned to provide reimbursement to any person damaged by the Notary's improper performance of official duties. (TGC, Sec. 406.010)

Filing the Bond. The bond must be submitted with the Notary commission application at the office of the Secretary of State — before the applicant begins the official duties of office. The Secretary of State may accept an electronic filing of the bond if an agreement has been made with the surety company. (TGC, Sec. 406.010)

Protects Public. The Notary bond protects the public from a Notary's misconduct or negligence. The bond does not protect the Notary, who is personally liable for all damages resulting from illegal or improper performance of notarial duties. (NPEM)

The bond's surety company agrees to pay damages totalling up to $10,000 to persons who suffer financially because of the Notary's improper acts, intentional or not, in the event the Notary does not have the financial resources to pay these damages. The surety may seek compensation from the Notary for any damages it has to pay out on the Notary's behalf.

Oath of Office

Requirement. Each prospective Notary must take and sign an oath of office in the presence of a Notary Public or other person authorized to administer oaths in Texas. This is the oath required by Section 1, Article XVI of the Texas Constitution. A Notary cannot execute his or her own oath of office. (TGC, Sec. 406.010)

Filing the Oath. The oath of office appears on the Notary commission and is not filed with the Secretary of State. (TGC, Sec. 406.005)

Jurisdiction

Statewide. Notaries may perform official acts throughout the state of Texas but not beyond the state borders. A Notary may not witness a signing outside Texas and then return to the state to perform the notarization; all parts of a notarial act must be performed at the same time and place within the state of Texas. (TGC, Sec. 406.003)

Term of Office

Four-Year Term. A Texas Notary Public's term of office is four years, ending at midnight on the commission expiration date. (TGC, Sec. 406.002)

Resignation

Procedure. To resign, a Notary must deliver his or her journal and public papers to the county clerk in the county in which the Notary resides. (TGC, Sec. 406.022)

The National Notary Association recommends that the Notary should also immediately notify the Secretary of State by certified mail and destroy his or her Notary seal. (See "Disposition of Notary Records," page 46.)

Change of Address

Notify Secretary of State. Whenever a Notary changes his or her address, the Notary must inform the Secretary of State of the address change within 10 days after the change. (TGC, Sec. 406.019)

Moving Out of State. If a Notary moves his or her residence out of Texas, he or she vacates the office of Notary. Such a move has the same effect as resignation. (See "Resignation," above.) (TGC, Sec. 406.020)

Ex Officio Notaries. An ex officio Notary — one who acquires notarial powers because of a particular office or position — who moves permanently from his or her assigned jurisdiction vacates the office of Notary Public. Such a move has the same effect as resignation. (See "Resignation," above.) (TGC, Sec. 406.021)

Change of Name

Procedure. A Notary may change the name on his or her Notary Public commission by submitting to the Secretary of State 1) a new application, 2) the original Notary commission, 3) a rider or endorsement from the bond agency or surety, and 4) a $20 filing fee. All four of these items must be sent at the same time. Instructions are available from the Notary Public Unit at 1-512-463-5705. (NPEM)

Exception. Texas law does not require Notaries to change the name on their current commission in the event they change their name due to marriage or other reason. But the Notary must continue to use the name on the current commission for all official acts and then change the commission name when he or she renews.

OFFICIAL NOTARIAL ACTS

Authorized Acts

Notaries may perform the following official acts: (TGC, Sec. 406.016 and TCPRC, Sec. 121.001)

- <u>Acknowledgments</u>, certifying that a signer personally appeared before the Notary, was identified by the Notary, and acknowledged freely signing the document. (See pages 22–26.)

- <u>Certified Copies</u>, guaranteeing that a photocopy of an original document not recordable in public records is true and complete. (See pages 26–28.)

- <u>Depositions</u>, certifying that the spoken words of a witness were accurately taken down in writing, though this act is most often done by skilled court reporters. (See pages 30–31.)

- <u>Jurats</u>, certifying that a signer personally appeared before the Notary, took an oath or affirmation from the Notary, and signed the document in the Notary's presence. (See pages 32–33.)

- <u>Oaths and Affirmations</u>, which are solemn promises to God (oaths) or solemn promises on one's own personal honor (affirmations). (See pages 33–34.)

- <u>Proofs of Acknowledgment by Handwriting</u>, in which witnesses appear before the Notary and swear to a deposition or affidavit that the signature of another person, the principal, is genuine. (See pages 34–36.)

- <u>Proofs of Acknowledgment by Subscribing Witness</u>, in which a subscribing witness personally appears and swears to the Notary that another person, the principal, signed a document. (Also called a proof of execution by subscribing witness.) (See pages 36–38.)

- <u>Protests</u>, certifying that a negotiable instrument or other written promise to pay, such as a bill of exchange, was not honored. (See pages 38–40.)

Unauthorized Acts

<u>Notary's Own Signature</u>. Notaries are not permitted to notarize their own signatures. (NPEM)

<u>Issue Identification</u>. Notaries are not permitted to issue an identification card. (TGC, Sec. 406.016)

<u>Marriages</u>. Texas Notaries are not authorized to perform marriages unless the Notary is also a member of the clergy or an official authorized to solemnize marriages.

<u>Telephone Notarizations</u>. Notarizations over the telephone are absolutely forbidden. A document signer *must* appear before the Notary, face to face in the same room, at the time of notarization, not before, not later. (NPEM)

In addition, notarization based on a Notary's recognition of a signature, or on the unsworn word of a third party, without the signer's appearance before the Notary is forbidden. (TGC, Sec. 406.009)

However, the *sworn* word of witnesses to the signing or acknowledging or of persons who can identify the signature by handwriting is permitted in special circumstances. (See "Proof of Acknowledgment by Subscribing Witness," pages 36–38 and "Proof of Acknowledgment by Handwriting," pages 34–36.)

Acknowledgments

<u>A Common Notarial Act</u>. Acknowledgments are one of the most common forms of notarization. Typically, they are executed on documents such as deeds and other documents affecting real property that will be publicly recorded by a County Recorder.

<u>Purpose</u>. In executing an acknowledgment, the Notary certifies three things: (TCPRC, Secs. 121.005 and 121.006)

1) The signer *personally appeared* before the Notary on the date and in the county indicated on the notarial certificate

(notarization cannot be based on a telephone call or on a Notary's familiarity with a signature); and

2) The signer was *positively identified* by the Notary through personal knowledge or other satisfactory evidence (see "Identifying Document Signers," pages 40–43); and

3) The signer *acknowledged* to the Notary that the signature was freely made for the purposes stated in the document. (If a document is willingly signed in the presence of the Notary, this tacit act can serve just as well as an oral statement of acknowledgment.)

<u>Certificates for Acknowledgments</u>. Texas law provides wording for an ordinary certificate of acknowledgment plus several short-form acknowledgment certificates that accommodate signers in various representative capacities and may be used as alternatives to other authorized certificates. (TCPRC, Secs. 121.007 and 121.008)

• Ordinary Certificate of Acknowledgment — wording must be substantially as follows:

```
State of Texas          )
                        ) ss.
County of _____ )
```

Before me _____ (name and title of officer [i.e.: Notary Public]) on this day personally appeared _____ (name[s] of signer[s]), known to me (or proved to me on the oath of _____ or through _____ [type of identification document]) to be the person(s) whose name(s) is/are subscribed to the foregoing instrument and acknowledged to me that he/she/they executed the same for the purposes and consideration therein expressed.

Given under my hand and seal of office this _____ day of _____, _____ (year).

_____ (Signature of Notary)   (Seal of Notary)

• Individual Acknowledgment Short-Form Certificate — for an individual or individuals signing on his, her or their own behalf:

```
State of Texas          )
                        ) ss.
County of _____ )
```

This instrument was acknowledged before me on _____ (date) by _____ (name of signer[s]).

_____ (Signature of Notary)   (Seal of Notary)

- **Attorney in Fact Acknowledgment Short-Form Certificate** — for an attorney in fact acting on behalf of a principal:

State of Texas   )
) ss.
County of _____)

This instrument was acknowledged before me on _____ (date) by _____ (name of attorney in fact) as attorney in fact for _____ (name of principal).

_____ (Signature of Notary)   (Seal of Notary)

- **Partnership Acknowledgment Short-Form Certificate** — for a partner or partners acting on behalf of a partnership:

State of Texas   )
) ss.
County of _____)

This instrument was acknowledged before me on _____ (date) by _____ (name[s] of partner[s]) on behalf of _____ (name of partnership), a partnership.

_____ (Signature of Notary)   (Seal of Notary)

- **Corporate Acknowledgment Short-Form Certificate** — for a corporate officer acting on behalf of a corporation:

State of Texas   )
) ss.
County of _____)

This instrument was acknowledged before me on _____ (date) by _____ (name of corporate officer), _____ (title of officer) of _____ (name of corporation acknowledging), a _____ (state of incorporation) corporation, on behalf of said corporation.

_____ (Signature of Notary)   (Seal of Notary)

- **Representative Acknowledgment Short-Form Certificate** — for a public officer, trustee, executor, administrator, guardian or other representative acting on behalf of an entity or person:

State of Texas   )
) ss.
County of _____)

This instrument was acknowledged before me on _____ (date) by _____ (name of representative), _____ (title of representation) of _____ (name of entity or person represented).

_____ (Signature of Notary)   (Seal of Notary)

Texas law also allows modification of the preceding certificates as circumstances require. The authorization by law of particular certificate wordings does not prohibit the use of other appropriate wordings. (TCPRC, Sec. 121.006)

Identification of Acknowledger. In executing an acknowledgment, the Notary must identify the signer through personal knowledge or another form of satisfactory evidence. (See "Identifying Document Signers," pages 40–43.) (TCPRC, Section 121.005)

Witnessing Signature not Required. For an acknowledgment, the document does *not* have to be signed in the Notary's presence. Rather, the document signer need only acknowledge having made the signature. As long as the signer appears before the Notary at the time of notarization to *acknowledge having signed*, the Notary may execute the acknowledgment. The document could have been signed an hour before, a week before, a year before, etc. — as long as the signer appears before the Notary with the signed document at the time of notarization to admit that the signature is his or her own. However, for a jurat notarization, requiring an oath or affirmation, the document indeed must be signed in the presence of the Notary. (See "Jurats," pages 32–33.)

Terminology. In discussing the notarial act of acknowledgment, it is important to use the proper terminology. A Notary *takes* or *executes* an acknowledgment, while a document signer *makes* or *gives* an acknowledgment.

Who May Take Acknowledgments. Besides Notaries, a clerk of a district court or a judge or clerk of a county court can take acknowledgments and proofs within Texas. (TCPRC, Sec. 121.001)

TEXAS NOTARY LAW PRIMER

Outside of Texas, but inside the United States and its jurisdictions, acknowledgments and proofs of execution may be executed by: (TCPRC, Sec. 121.001)

1) Notaries of other U.S. states and jurisdictions;

2) Clerks of courts of record having a seal; and

3) Commissioners of deeds appointed under the laws of Texas.

Outside of the United States and its jurisdictions, acknowledgments and proofs of execution may be executed by: (TCPRC, Sec. 121.001)

1) A Notary Public or other official authorized to administer oaths in the given jurisdiction;

2) A minister, commissioner or charge d'affaires of the United States who is a resident of and is accredited in the given foreign country; and

3) A consul general, consul, vice-consul, commercial agent, vice-commercial agent, deputy consul or consular agent of the United States who is residing in the given foreign country.

A commissioned officer of the U.S. Armed Forces (or of a U.S. Armed Forces Auxiliary) may take acknowledgments or proofs of execution from a member of the armed forces, a member of an armed forces auxiliary, or a member's spouse. (See "Military-Officer Notarizations," page 59.) (TCPRC, Sec. 121.001)

Certified Copies

Purpose. Texas Notaries have authority to certify that a copy of an original document is a complete and true reproduction of the document that was copied. The Notary's authority to certify copies is limited to documents which are *not* public records or recordable in the public record. (TGC, Sec. 406.016)

Notaries may also certify copies of entries in their own official journals of notarial acts. (See "Certified Copies of Notarial Records," page 28.) (TGC, Sec. 406.014)

Procedure. The permanent custodian of the original document

must present it to the Notary and request a certified copy. The Notary makes *two* photocopies — one for certification and one for the Notary's official records. (NPEM)

A common request is to certify a copy of a college diploma, since only one such document exists and most people do not want to risk parting with the original when proof of their graduate status is requested by a prospective employer or school.

Precautions. Though a transcription or hand-rendered copy is not expressly prohibited, the NNA strongly recommends that Notaries only certify photocopies, to avert the high likelihood that something may be inadvertently omitted or mistranscribed in a handmade copy. And, to minimize the opportunity for fraud, the making of the photocopy should be done by the Notary. Otherwise, the Notary should carefully compare the copy to the original, word for word, to ensure that it is complete and identical.

Copy Certification of Recordable Documents Prohibited. Texas Notaries are prohibited from certifying copies of recordable documents. A document does not have to be recorded, but merely *recordable* for the Notary to be prohibited from making a certified copy. (NPEM)

Copy Certification of Vital Records Prohibited. Texas Notaries are expressly prohibited from certifying copies of birth or death certificates, because these are *recordable* documents. Only officials in a bureau of vital statistics or other public record office may certify originals or copies of such certificates. (See "Bureaus of Vital Statistics," pages 108–112.) A Notary's "certification" of such a copy may lend credibility to what is actually a counterfeit or altered document. (TGC, Sec. 406.016)

Copies Certified by County Clerk. A county clerk may certify a copy of a notarial record or notarized document filed with that county clerk. A copy certified in this manner has the same authority as if it was certified by the Notary who kept the record or performed the notarization. (TGC, Sec. 406.015)

Certificate for Certified Copy. The Secretary of State provides the following sample certificate wording for certifying a copy of a non-recordable document: (NPEM)

TEXAS NOTARY LAW PRIMER

State of Texas)
) ss.
County of _____)

On this _____ day of _____, 19 _____, I certify that the preceding or attached document, and the duplicate retained by me as a notarial record, are true, exact, complete and unaltered photocopies made by me of _____ (description of original document), presented to me by the document's custodian, _____ (name of original document's custodian), and that, to the best of my knowledge, the photocopied document is neither a public record nor a publicly recordable document, certified copies of which are available from an official source other than a Notary.

_____ (Signature of Notary)   (Seal of Notary)

Certified Copies of Notarial Records

<u>Procedure</u>. Members of the public may lawfully request Notary-certified photocopies of entries in the Notary's official journal or any notarial record in the Notary's office. (TGC, Sec. 406.014)

Only photocopies — never hand-rendered duplications — of notarial records should be certified by a Notary. The notarial certificate should be attached to the front of the photocopy or copies, in contrast to loose acknowledgment certificates that usually are attached to a document's last page.

To prevent unauthorized viewing of notarial records, the careful Notary will only show and provide copies of entries or official papers in response to a written request that includes the signer(s) name(s), type of document, month and year of notarization. In addition, the National Notary Association recommends that the individual requesting the notarial-record copy should be positively identified and sign in the Notary's record book.

<u>Certificate for Certified Copy of Notarial Record</u>. The Secretary of State provides the following sample certificate wording for certifying a copy of an entry or page from the Notary's journal or other notarial record in the Notary's office: (NPEM)

State of Texas)
) ss.
County of _____)

On this _____ day of _____, 19 _____, I certify that the preceding or attached document, and the duplicate retained by me as a notarial record, are true, exact, complete and unaltered photocopies made by me of _____ (description of journal entry), held in my custody as a notarial record, and that, to the best of my knowledge, the photocopied document is neither a public record nor a publicly recordable document, certified copies of which are available from an official source other than a Notary.

_____ (Signature of Notary)   (Seal of Notary)

Copy Certification by Document Custodian

Purpose. While not an official notarial act, copy certification by document custodian *may* serve as an alternative to a Notary-certified document copy when it would be inappropriate for anyone but the document's permanent holder to certify the copy.

It should be noted that copy certification by document custodian may not always be an acceptable substitute for a Notary-certified copy, so the person requesting the act should check to be sure it will serve the required purposes.

Notary Executes a Jurat. The permanent keeper of the document — the document custodian — certifies the copy, *not* the Notary. The document custodian makes a photocopy of the original document; makes a written statement about the trueness, correctness and completeness of the copy; signs that statement before a Notary; and takes an oath or affirmation regarding the truth of the statement. The Notary, having witnessed the signing and given the oath or affirmation, executes a jurat.

Certificate for Copy Certification by Document Custodian. Copy certification by document custodian is, for the Notary's purposes, simply a jurat. The custodian's statement is not prescribed by law. The National Notary Association recommends the following wording, including the jurat:

State of Texas   )
) ss.
County of _____)

I, _____ (name of custodian of original document), hereby swear (or affirm) that the attached reproduction of _____ (description of original document) is a true, correct and complete photocopy of a document in my possession.

_____ (signature of custodian) _____ (address)

Subscribed and sworn to (or affirmed) before me this _____ day of _____, 19 _____, by _____ (name of custodian).

_____ (Signature of Notary)   (Seal of Notary)

Depositions and Affidavits

Purpose. A deposition is a signed transcript of the signer's oral statements taken down for use in a judicial proceeding. The deposition signer is called the *deponent*.

An affidavit is a signed statement made under oath or affirmation by a person called an *affiant*, and it is used for a variety of purposes both in and out of court.

For both a deposition and an affidavit, the Notary must administer an oath or affirmation and complete some form of jurat, which the Notary signs and seals.

Depositions. With a deposition, both sides in a lawsuit or court case have the opportunity to question the deponent. The questions and answers are transcribed into a written statement, then signed and sworn to before an oath-administering official.

Texas Notaries have the power to take depositions — meaning, to transcribe the words spoken aloud by a deponent — but this duty is most often executed by trained and certified shorthand reporters, also known as court reporters. (TGC, Sec. 406.016)

Affidavits. Affidavits are used in and out of court for a variety of purposes, from declaring losses to an insurance company to declaring U.S. citizenship before traveling to a foreign country. An affidavit is a document containing a statement voluntarily signed and sworn to (or affirmed) before a Notary or other oath-administering official. If used in a judicial proceeding, only one side in the case need participate in the affidavit process, in contrast to the deposition.

In an affidavit, the Notary's certificate typically sandwiches the affiant's signed statement, with the venue and affiant's name at the top of the document and the jurat wording at the end. The Notary is responsible for the venue, affiant's name and any notarial text at the beginning and end of the affidavit, and the affiant is responsible for the signed statement in the middle.

Certificate for Depositions. The Secretary of State provides the following sample certificate wording for depositions: (NPEM)

- Certificate for deposition in response to written questions:

    The State of Texas   )
    County of _____)

NOTARY LAWS EXPLAINED

_____ (Plaintiff)   ) In the _____Court
           v.   ) of _____ County, Texas
_____ (Defendant)   ) Cause No. _____

I hereby certify that the foregoing answers of _____, the witness forenamed, were signed and sworn to before me on _____ (date), by said witness.

_____ (Signature of Notary)   (Seal of Notary)

- **Certificate for deposition in response to oral questions:**

The State of Texas   )
County of _____)

_____ (Plaintiff)   ) In the _____Court
           v.   ) of _____ County, Texas
_____ (Defendant)   ) Cause No. _____

I, _____ (Notary Public's name), Notary Public in _____ County, Texas, do hereby certify that the said witness _____ (name) was first sworn to testify the truth and nothing but the truth; that he/she was then carefully examined; that his/her testimony which is above given was by me reduced to writing (or typewriting) (or to writing or typewriting by _____ (name), a person under my personal supervision; or by the deponent himself/herself in my presence) and by no other person, and that after it had been so reduced to writing (or typewriting) subscribed by the deponent before me all on _____ day of _____, _____ (year).

_____ (Signature of Notary)   (Seal of Notary)

<u>Certificate for Affidavits</u>. Affidavits require jurat certificates. (See "Jurats," pages 31–32.)

<u>Oath (Affirmation) for Depositions and Affidavits</u>. If no other wording is prescribed, a Notary may use the following language in administering an oath (affirmation) for an affidavit or deposition:

> Do you solemnly swear that the statements made in this affidavit (or deposition) are the truth, the whole truth, and nothing but the truth, so help you God?

> (Do you solemnly affirm that the statements made in this affidavit [or deposition] are the truth, the whole truth, and nothing but the truth?)

For both oath and affirmation, the affiant must respond aloud and affirmatively, with "I do" or "Yes" or the like.

Jurats

<u>Part of Verification</u>. In notarizing affidavits, depositions and other forms of written verification requiring an oath by the signer, the Notary typically executes a jurat.

<u>Purpose</u>. While the purpose of an acknowledgment is to positively identify a document signer, the purpose of a verification with jurat is to compel truthfulness by appealing to the signer's conscience and fear of criminal penalties for perjury.
In executing a jurat, a Notary certifies that:

1) The signer *personally appeared* before the Notary at the time of notarization on the date and in the county indicated (notarization based on a telephone call or on familiarity with a signature is not acceptable); and

2) The Notary *watched the signature* being made at the time of notarization; and

3) The Notary *administered an oath* or affirmation to the signer.

<u>Certificate for a Jurat</u>. A typical jurat is the wording, "Subscribed and sworn to (or affirmed) before me on this _____ (date) by _____ (name of signer)..." or similar language. "Subscribed" means "signed." The Secretary of State provides the following jurat wording: (NPEM)

    State of Texas   )
) ss.
    County of _____)

    Sworn to and subscribed before me the _____ day of _____, _____ (year).

    _____ (Signature of Notary)   (Seal of Notary)

<u>Identification</u>. When executing a jurat, the prudent Notary will positively identify each signer, even though identification is not required by law for a jurat as it is for an acknowledgment.

<u>Wording for Jurat Oath (Affirmation)</u>. If not otherwise prescribed by law, a Texas Notary may use the following or similar wording to administer an oath (or affirmation) in conjunction with a jurat:

Do you solemnly swear that the statements in this document are true to the best of your knowledge and belief, so help you God?

(Do you solemnly affirm that the statements in this document are true to the best of your knowledge and belief?)

Oaths and Affirmations

Purpose. An oath is a solemn, spoken pledge to a Supreme Being. An affirmation is a solemn, spoken pledge on one's own personal honor, with no reference to a Supreme Being. Both are usually a promise or pledge of truthfulness or fidelity and have the same legal effect. In taking an oath or affirmation in an official proceeding, a person may be subject to criminal penalties for perjury should he or she fail to be truthful.

An oath or affirmation can be a full-fledged notarial act in its own right, as when giving an oath of office to a public official (when "swearing in" a public official), or it can be part of the process of notarizing a document (e.g., executing a jurat or swearing in a credible identifying witness).

A person who objects to taking an oath — pledging to a Supreme Being — may instead be given an affirmation, which does not refer to a Supreme Being.

Power to Administer. Texas Notaries and certain other officers are authorized to administer oaths and affirmations. (TGC, Sec. 406.016)

Wording for Oath (Affirmation). If law does not dictate otherwise, a Texas Notary may use the following or similar words in administering an oath (or affirmation):

- Oath (affirmation) for an affiant signing an affidavit or a deponent signing a deposition:

    Do you solemnly swear that the statements in this document are true to the best of your knowledge and belief, so help you God?

    (Do you solemnly affirm that the statements in this document are true to the best of your knowledge and belief?)

- Oath (affirmation) for a credible identifying witness identifying a document signer who is in the Notary's presence:

    Do you solemnly swear that you personally know this signer truly holds the identity he (or she) claims, so help you God?

(Do you solemnly affirm that you personally know this signer truly holds the identity he [or she] claims?)

- Oath (affirmation) for a subscribing witness identifying a document signer who is not in the Notary's presence:

Do you solemnly swear that you saw (name of the document signer) sign his/her name to this document or that he/she acknowledged to you having executed it for the purposes and consideration therein stated, and that you signed the document at the request of (name of the document signer), so help you God?

(Do you solemnly affirm that you saw [name of the document signer] sign his/her name to this document or that he/she acknowledged to you having executed it for the purposes and consideration therein stated, and that you signed the document at the request of [name of the document signer]?)

The oath or affirmation wording must be spoken aloud, and the person taking the oath or affirmation must answer affirmatively with, "I do," "Yes," or the like. A nod or grunt is not a clear and sufficient response. If a person is mute and unable to speak, the Notary may rely on written notes to communicate.

Ceremony and Gestures. To impress upon the oath- or affirmation-taker the importance of truthfulness, the Notary is encouraged to lend a sense of ceremony and formality to the oath or affirmation. During administration of an oath or affirmation, the Notary and document signer traditionally raise their right hands, though this is not a legal requirement. Notaries generally have discretion to use words and gestures they feel will most compellingly appeal to the conscience of the oath-taker or affirmant.

Proof of Acknowledgment by Handwriting

Purpose. In very limited situations, a proof of acknowledgment by handwriting may be taken. To do so, two witnesses, who are well acquainted with the handwriting of an unavailable principal signer, must personally appear and swear by deposition or affidavit that the signature of the principal signer is genuine. (TCPRC, Sec. 121.011)

In addition, the signature of at least one witness who signed the document must also be similarly proved. If the principal signer signed by mark, then the signatures of at least two witnesses to the mark must be similarly proved. (TCPRC, Sec. 121.011)

Requirements for Use. The execution of a document may be proved by handwriting *only* if: (TCPRC, Sec. 121.011)

1) The signer of the document and all of the witnesses are deceased;

2) The signer and all of the witnesses are not Texas residents;

3) The residences of the signer and all of the witnesses are unknown to the person seeking to prove execution of the document and cannot be ascertained;

4) The witnesses have become legally incompetent to testify; or

5) The signer refuses to acknowledge the execution of the document and all of the witnesses are deceased, not residents of Texas, legally incompetent or their places of residence are unknown.

In Lieu of Acknowledgment. On recordable documents, a proof of acknowledgment by handwriting is regarded as an acceptable substitute for an acknowledgment. (TCPRC, Sec. 121.011)

Witnesses. Two disinterested witnesses are required to establish proof of a signature. These witnesses must personally know the signer, must be well acquainted with the signer's handwriting, and must be able to recognize the signature as genuine. (TCPRC, Secs. 121.011)

Depositions or Affidavits Required. The witnesses to a proof of acknowledgment by handwriting must give evidence in the form of a deposition or affidavit which must satisfactorily prove to the Notary each requirement — that they are disinterested witnesses, that they personally know the signer, that they are well acquainted with the signer's handwriting, and that they determine the signature to be genuine.
The Notary must certify the witnesses' testimony and attach a certificate with the Notary's official seal, along with the depositions or affidavits of the witnesses to the document. (TCPRC, Sec. 121.011)

Certificate for Proof of Acknowledgment by Handwriting. A

sample certificate for proof of acknowledgment by handwriting is not prescribed by law. Since such acts are extremely rare and complex, the National Notary Association recommends that Notaries perform proofs of acknowledgment by handwriting only under the supervision of an attorney who would prepare the required certificates.

Oath (Affirmation) for Handwriting Witness. An acceptable oath for the witness might be:

> Do you solemnly swear that you personally know (name of signer), that you are well acquainted with (name of signer)'s handwriting, that you determine the signature on (description of document) to be that of (name of signer), and that you have no personal beneficial or financial interest in the document, so help you God?

> (Do you solemnly affirm that you personally know [name of signer], that you are well acquainted with [name of signer]'s handwriting, that you determine the signature on [description of document] to be that of [name of signer], and that you have no personal beneficial or financial interest in the document?)

Subpoena of Witness. Notaries may issue a subpoena — though this power is rarely used — to require the appearance of a witness to a document to testify about its execution. (See "Subpoena of Witness," page 38.) (TCPRC, Secs. 121.003 and 121.013)

Proof of Acknowledgment by Subscribing Witness

Purpose. In executing a proof of acknowledgment by subscribing witness (also called a proof of execution by a subscribing witness), a Notary certifies that the signature of a person who does not appear before the Notary — the principal signer — is genuine and freely made based on the sworn testimony of another person who does appear — a subscribing (signing) witness.

Proofs of acknowledgment by a subscribing witness are used when the principal signer is out of town or otherwise unavailable to appear before a Notary. Proofs should never be used because the principal signer prefers not to take the time to personally appear before a Notary. Because of the proof's high potential for fraud, it should be used only when there is no other option.

In Lieu of Acknowledgment. On recordable documents, a proof of acknowledgment by subscribing witness is regarded as an acceptable substitute for an acknowledgement. (TCPRC, Sec. 121.009)

Subscribing Witness. A subscribing witness is a person who watches a principal sign a document (or who personally takes the principal's acknowledgment) and then subscribes (signs) his or her own name on the document at the principal's request. This witness brings that document to a Notary on the principal's behalf and takes an oath or affirmation from the Notary to the effect that the principal did indeed willingly sign (or acknowledge signing) the document and request the witness to also sign the document. (TCPRC, Sec. 121.009)

The ideal subscribing witness personally knows the principal signer and has no personal beneficial or financial interest in the document or transaction. It would be foolish of the Notary, for example, to rely on the word of a subscribing witness presenting for notarization a power of attorney that names this very witness as attorney in fact.

Identifying Subscribing Witness. The subscribing witness *must* be personally known to the Notary or the identity must be proved on the oath of a credible identifying witness who is personally known to the Notary. (TCPRC, Sec. 121.009)

Certificate for Proof of Acknowledgment by Subscribing Witness. Texas law specifies the following certificate (sometimes called a "witness jurat") or substantially similar wording for a proof of acknowledgment by a subscribing witness: (TCPRC, Sec. 121.010)

State of Texas   )
) ss.
County of _____)

Before me _____ (name and title of officer [i.e., Notary Public]), on this day personally appeared _____ (name of subscribing witness), known to me (or proved to me on the oath of _____ [name of credible identifying witness]) to be the person whose name is subscribed as a witness to the foregoing instrument of writing, and after being duly sworn by me stated on oath that he/she saw _____ (name of principal signer), the grantor or person who executed the foregoing instrument, subscribe the same (or that the grantor or person who executed such instrument of writing acknowledged in his/her presence that he/she had executed the same for the purposes and consideration therein expressed), and that he/she had signed the same as a witness at the request of the grantor (or person who executed the same).

Given under my hand and seal of office this _____ day of _____, 19 _____ A.D.

_____ (Signature of Notary)   (Seal of Notary)

<u>Oath (Affirmation) for Subscribing Witness</u>. An acceptable oath for the subscribing witness might be:

> Do you solemnly swear that you saw (name of the document signer) sign his/her name to this document or that he/she acknowledged to you having executed it for the purposes and consideration therein stated, and that you signed the document at the request of (name of the document signer), so help you God?
>
> (Do you solemnly affirm that you saw [name of the document signer] sign his/her name to this document or that he/she acknowledged to you having executed it for the purposes and consideration therein stated, and that you signed the document at the request of [name of the document signer]?)

<u>Journal</u>. It is recommended that the subscribing witness then sign the Notary's journal.

<u>Interpreters</u>. In a proceeding to prove the execution of a document, Notaries have the authority to employ and swear interpreters. A Notary may not personally serve as an interpreter in a translation in which the Notary would have to administer an oath to the interpreter. (TCPRC, Sec. 121.003)

<u>Subpoena of Witness</u>. Though this power is rarely used, Texas Notaries may issue a subpoena to require the appearance of a witness to a document to testify about its execution. The person who wants the document proven must submit a sworn application stating that a witness refuses to appear and testify about the document's execution and that the document cannot be proven without the witness's testimony. A witness may not be required to leave his or her county of residence, but if temporarily in the county where the proof is sought, the witness may then be required to appear. (TCPRC, Secs. 121.003 and 121.013)

Protests

<u>Purpose</u>. In rare instances, Texas Notaries may be asked to protest a negotiable instrument for nonpayment. A protest is a

written statement by a Notary or other authorized officer verifying that payment was not received on an instrument such as a bank draft. Failure to pay is called *dishonor*. Before issuing a certificate of protest, the Notary must present the bank draft or other instrument to the person, firm or institution obliged to pay, a procedure called *presentment*. (TGC, Sec. 406.016)

Antiquated Act. In the 19th century, protests were common notarial acts in the United States, but they rarely are performed today due to the advent of modern electronic communications and resulting changes in our banking and financial systems. Modern Notaries most often encounter protests in the context of international commerce.

Special Knowledge Required. Notarial acts of protest are complicated and varied, requiring a special knowledge of financial and legal terminology. Only Notaries who have the requisite special knowledge, or who are acting under the supervision of an experienced bank officer or an attorney familiar with the Uniform Commercial Code, should attempt a protest.

Certificate for Protest. The Secretary of State provides the following certificate wording for a protest: (NPEM)

(Insert bill or note or copy thereof)

United States of America)
State of Texas) ss.
County of _____)

Be it known that on the _____ day of _____, ____ (year), at the request of _____ (name of person appearing before Notary), of _____ (name of person or entity represented), I _____ (name of Notary), a Notary Public duly commissioned and sworn, residing in _____ County, Texas, did present the original _____ (description of instrument) hereto attached for $_____, with accrued interest thereon of $_____, dated _____, ____ (year), and demanded payment (or acceptance) thereof which was refused.

Whereupon I, at the request of the aforesaid _____ (name of person appearing before Notary), did protest and by these presents do protest, as well against the drawer, maker, endorsers, and acceptors of said instruments as against all others, whom it may concern, for exchange, costs, charges, damages, and interest already incurred and hereinafter to be incurred by reason of non-payment thereof. I further certify that on _____, 19 ____, notice in writing of the foregoing presentment, demand, refusal and protest was given by

_____ (persons and status) by depositing notices thereof in the post office at _____, Texas, postage paid, directed as follows: _____. I further certify that notices were left as follows:

Notice left for _____ (name) at _____ (address)
Notice left for _____ (name) at _____ (address)

(Each of the named places the reputed place of residence of the person for whom the notice was left.)

In testimony whereof I have hereunto set my hand and affixed my seal of office at _____ (county), Texas, on _____ day of _____, ____ (year).

_____ (Signature of Notary)   (Seal of Notary)

PRACTICES AND PROCEDURES

Identifying Document Signers

Acknowledgments. In taking acknowledgments for any document, Texas law requires the Notary to identify the acknowledger. The following three methods of identification are acceptable, any one of which is considered satisfactory evidence of identity: (TCPRC, Sec. 121.005)

1) The Notary's *personal knowledge* of the signer's identity (see "Personal Knowledge of Identity," page 41);

2) The oath or affirmation of a personally known *credible identifying witness* (see "Credible Identifying Witnesses," pages 41–42); or

3) Reliable, current *identification documents* or ID cards (see "Identification Documents," pages 42–43).

Identification for Other Notarial Acts. While the law specifies identification standards only for acknowledgers, the prudent and conscientious Notary will apply these same standards in identifying any signer, whether for an acknowledgment or a jurat.

Capacity. Texas law is not clear on whether Notaries are required to *verify* the capacity in which a person signs. However, the law does state that for an acknowledgment by a person acting in a representative capacity — such as corporate officer, trustee, partner to a partnership, attorney in fact, or other capacity — the signer must personally appear before the Notary and acknowledge executing the instrument by proper authority in the capacity claimed for the purposes stated in the document. (TCPRC, Sec. 121.006)

Personal Knowledge of Identity

Definition. The safest and most reliable method of identifying a document signer is for the Notary to depend on his or her own personal knowledge of the signer's identity. Personal knowledge means familiarity with an individual resulting from interactions with that person over a period of time sufficient to eliminate every reasonable doubt that the person has the identity claimed.

Texas law does not specify how long a Notary must be acquainted with an individual before personal knowledge of identity may be claimed. So, the Notary's common sense must prevail. In general, the longer the Notary is acquainted with a person, and the more random interactions the Notary has had with that person, the more likely the individual is indeed personally known.

For instance, the Notary might safely regard a friend since childhood as personally known, but would be foolish to consider a person met for the first time the previous day as such. Whenever the Notary has a reasonable doubt about a signer's identity, that individual should not be considered personally known, and the identification should be made through either a credible identifying witness or reliable identification documents. (TCPRC, Sec. 121.005)

Credible Identifying Witnesses

Purpose. When a document signer is not personally known to the Notary and is not able to present reliable ID cards, that signer may be identified on the oath (or affirmation) of a credible identifying witness.

Qualifications. A credible identifying witness must be personally known to the Notary and the document signer personally known to the credible identifying witness. (See "Personal Knowledge of Identity," preceding.) There should be a chain of personal knowledge linking the Notary to the credible identifying witness to the signer. In a sense, a credible identifying witness is a walking, talking ID card. (TCPRC, Sec. 121.005)

A reliable credible identifying witness should have a reputation for honesty. The witness should be a competent individual who would not be tricked, cajoled, bullied or otherwise influenced into identifying someone he or she does not really know. And the witness, ideally, should have no personal beneficial or financial interest in the transaction requiring a notarial act.

Oath (Affirmation) for Credible Identifying Witness. An oath or affirmation must be administered to the credible identifying witness by the Notary to compel truthfulness.

If not otherwise prescribed by law, a Texas Notary may use the following or similar wording to administer an oath (or affirmation) to credible identifying witnesses:

> Do you solemnly swear that you know the signer truly holds the identity he (or she) claims?
>
> (Do you solemnly affirm that you know the signer truly holds the identity he [or she] claims?)

Journal Entry. Each credible identifying witness's name and residence address must be recorded in the Notary's journal. Prudent Notaries will also ask witnesses to sign the journal. (TGC, Sec. 406.014)

Not a Subscribing Witness. Do not confuse a *credible identifying* witness with a *subscribing* witness. A credible identifying witness vouches for the identity of a signer who appears before the Notary. A subscribing witness vouches for the genuineness of the signature of a signer who does not appear before the Notary. (See "Proof of Acknowledgment by Subscribing Witness," page 38.)

Identification Documents (ID Cards)

Acceptable Identification Documents. Texas requires that an identifying document or card relied on by a Notary to identify a stranger must be current and issued by a federal or state governmental agency and must contain a photograph and signature of the bearer. (TCPRC, Sec. 121.005 and NPEM)

Among the IDs authorized for use by Texas Notaries are state driver's and official nondriver's IDs, U.S. passports, U.S. military IDs, and resident alien IDs or "green cards" issued by the U.S. Immigration and Naturalization Service.

The National Notary Association urges Notaries to rely only

on IDs with a photograph, a physical description (e.g., "brown hair, green eyes") and a signature of the bearer. Most government-issued IDs contain all three components.

Unacceptable Identification Documents. Easily counterfeited Social Security cards, birth certificates and credit cards are worthless as primary identifying documents.

Multiple Identification. While one good identification document or card is sufficient to identify a signer, the Notary may ask for more.

Fraudulent Identification. Identification documents are the least secure of the three methods of identifying a document signer, because phony ID cards are common. The Notary should scrutinize each card for evidence of tampering or counterfeiting, or for evidence that it is a genuine card issued to an impostor.

Some clues that an ID card may have been fraudulently tampered with include: mismatched type styles, a photograph raised from the surface, a signature that does not match the signature on the document, unauthorized lamination of the card, and smudges, erasures, smears or discolorations.

Possible tip-offs to a counterfeit ID card include: misspelled words, a brand new-looking card with an old date of issuance, two cards with exactly the same photograph, and inappropriate patterns and textures.

Some possible indications that a card may have been issued to an impostor include: the card's birth date or address is unknown to the bearer, all the ID cards seem brand new, and the bearer is unwilling to leave a thumbprint in the journal. (Such a print is not a requirement of law but is requested by some Notaries as protection against forgers and lawsuits. Refusal to leave a thumbprint is not in itself grounds to deny a notarization.)

Journal of Notarial Acts

Requirement. Texas Notaries are required to make a record in a Notary journal of *every* document notarized. It is strongly recommended that the journal or recordbook be a permanently bound recordbook (not loose-leaf) with preprinted page numbers. (TGC, Sec. 406.014 and TCPRC, Sec. 121.012)

Court Clerk Exemption. A court clerk, notarizing documents for the court, is not required to keep a journal. (TGC, Sec. 406.014)

Journal Entries. For each notarization, the journal must contain the following entries: (TGC, Sec. 406.014)

1) The date of each document notarized;

2) The date on which the notarization was performed;

3) The name of the signer, grantor or maker;

4) The signer's, grantor's or maker's residence address;

5) A statement of how the signer, grantor or maker was identified (If by personal knowledge, the journal notation would read, "Personal Knowledge." If by introduction through a credible identifying witness, the notation would be "Credible Identifying Witness," followed by the witness's name and residence address. If by an ID card or document, the following would be recorded: type of ID and its issuing agency, serial or identification number, and date of issuance or expiration.);

6) In the case of a proof of acknowledgment by subscribing witness, the residence address of the witness and whether the witness was personally known or introduced by a credible identifying witness (if introduced by a credible identifying witness, also include the credible identifying witness's name and residence address);

7) The name and residence address of the grantee (the recipient of the property), if applicable;

8) If land is conveyed or charged, the name and residence address of the original grantee and the county where the land is located; and

9) A brief description of the document (the title or type of the document or proceeding — e.g., grant deed, affidavit of support, oath of office, etc.).

Entry for Fees. Notaries must keep a fee book — a record of

the fees charged for notarial services — which shall be subject to public inspection at any time. This fee book may be the same book as the Notary journal, with the fees charged included with other journal entries. (TGC, Sec. 603.006 and NPEM)

Additional Entries. Notaries may include additional information in their journals that is pertinent to a given notarization. Many Notaries, for example, ask for a signature in the Notary journal as proof the signer personally appeared and as a deterrence to fraud. And many also enter the telephone numbers of signers and witnesses as well as the address where the notarization was performed, if not at the Notary's office. A description of the document signer's demeanor (e.g., "The signer appeared very nervous") or notations about the identity of other persons who were present for the notarization may also be pertinent.

One important entry to include is the signer's representative capacity — attorney in fact, trustee, guardian, corporate officer or other capacity — if not signing on his or her own behalf.

Increasingly, Notaries are asking document signers to leave a thumbprint in the journal as a deterrence to fraud, since no forger wants to leave a print behind as evidence of an attempted crime. A thumbprint also offers indisputable proof that a person did or did not appear.

Inspection of Notarial Records. Since the Notary's official journal is kept for the public benefit, members of the public may lawfully request to examine it. (TGC, Sec. 406.014)

The careful Notary will only show and provide copies of entries in response to a written request that includes the signer(s) name(s), type of document, month and year of notarization. In addition, the National Notary Association recommends that the individual requesting the notarial-record copy should be positively identified and sign in the Notary's record book.

Although the journal may be inspected, the Notary should never be relaxed about its security. Any inspection must be performed in the Notary's presence. No one should be allowed to take possession of the journal, even for just a few minutes.

Copy of Journal Entry. Notaries are permitted to certify copies of entries in their own official journals or any record in their office and to charge 50¢ for each page certified in addition to the $6 fee for the certificate. (TGC, Sec. 406.014 and 406.024)

The Secretary of State provides the following sample certificate wording for certifying a copy of an entry or page from the Notary's journal or other record in the Notary's office: (NPEM)

State of Texas   )
) ss.
County of _____)

On this _____ day of _____, 19 _____, I certify that the preceding or attached document, and the duplicate retained by me as a notarial record, are true, exact, complete and unaltered photocopies made by me of _____ (description of journal entry), held in my custody as a notarial record, and that, to the best of my knowledge, the photocopied document is neither a public record nor a publicly recordable document, certified copies of which are available from an official source other than a Notary.

_____ (Signature of Notary)   (Seal of Notary)

<u>Never Surrender Journal</u>. Notaries should never surrender control of their official journals to anyone, unless expressly subpoenaed by a court order. Even when an employer has paid for the Notary's official journal and seal, they go with the Notary upon termination of employment; no person but the Notary can lawfully possess and use these official adjuncts of office.

<u>Disposition of Notary Records</u>. Upon resignation, death or removal from the office, the Notary, or his or her representative, must deposit the Notary's journal with the clerk of the county where the Notary resides or resided. (TGC, Sec. 406.022)

Notarial Certificate

<u>Requirement</u>. In notarizing any document, a Notary must complete a notarial certificate. The certificate is wording that indicates exactly what the Notary has certified. The notarial certificate may be typed or printed on the document itself or on an attachment to it. The certificate should contain:

1) A *venue* indicating where the notarization is being performed. "State of Texas, County of _____," is the typical venue wording, with the appropriate county inserted in the blank. The letters "SS." or "SCT." sometimes appear after the venue; they abbreviate the Latin word *scilicet*, meaning "in particular" or "namely."

2) A *statement of particulars* which indicates what the notarization has certified. An acknowledgment certificate would include such wording as: "This instrument was acknowledged before me on _____ (date) by _____ (name of signer)." A jurat certificate would include such wording as: "Signed and sworn to (or affirmed) before me on _____ (date) by _____ (name of signer)."

3) A *testimonium clause*, which may be optional if the date is included in the statement of particulars: "Witness my hand and official seal, this _____ day of _____, 19____." In this phrase, the Notary formally attests to the truthfulness of the preceding facts in the certificate. "Hand" means signature.

4) The *official signature of the Notary*, exactly as the name appears on the commission certificate and on the Notary's official seal.

5) The *official seal of the Notary*. On many certificates, the letters "L.S." appear, indicating where the Notary's seal is to be placed. These letters abbreviate the Latin term *locus sigilli*, meaning "place of the seal." An inking seal should be placed near but not over the letters, so that wording imprinted by the seal or stamp will not be obscured. An embossing seal may be placed directly over the letters — slightly displacing portions of the characters and leaving a clue that document examiners can use to distinguish an original from a counterfeit photocopy.

<u>Loose Certificates</u>. When appropriate certificate wording is not preprinted on the document for the Notary to fill out, a loose certificate may be attached. Normally, this form is stapled to the document's left margin on the signature page. Only one side of the certificate should be stapled, so it can be lifted to view the document beneath it.

To prevent a loose certificate from being removed and fraudulently placed on another document, there are precautions a Notary can take. For instance, the Notary can write a brief description of the document on the certificate: e.g., "This certificate is attached to a _____ (title or type of document), dated _____, of _____ (number) pages, also signed by _____ (name[s] of other signer[s])."

While fraud-deterrent steps such as this one can make it much more difficult for a loose certificate to be removed and misused, there is no absolute protection against removal and misuse. Notaries, however, must absolutely ensure that while a certificate remains in their control, it is attached only to its intended document. A Notary must never give or mail a signed and stamped notarial certificate to another person and trust that person to attach it to a particular document; this would be an indefensible action in a civil court of law.

Do Not Pre-Sign/Seal Certificates. A Notary should *never* sign or seal certificates ahead of time or permit other persons to attach loose notarial certificates to documents. Nor should the Notary send an unattached, signed and sealed, loose certificate through the mail, even if requested to do so by a signer who previously appeared before the Notary. These actions may facilitate fraud or forgery, and they could subject the Notary to lawsuits to recover damages resulting from the Notary's neglect or misconduct.

Notary Seal

Requirement. A Texas Notary must affix an impression of an official seal on the certificate portion of every document notarized. (TGC, Sec. 406.013)

Format. The seal may either be circular, not more than two inches in diameter, or rectangular, not more than an inch in height and two and one-half inches in length. The seal must have a serrated or milled-edge border. (TGC, Sec. 406.013)

Stamp or Embosser. The seal must print in ink or emboss a photographically reproducible impression. A hand-drawn seal is not acceptable. (TGC, Sec. 406.013)
Because the image must be photocopiable, most Notaries use an inked rubber stamp seal, since an embossment would have to be smudged or darkened to be picked up by microfilm. An embosser may be used *in addition* to the required photographically reproducible seal, but it must not be used over this seal nor over the Notary's signature.

Required Information. The Notary seal must contain the following elements: (TGC, Sec. 406.013)

- Name of the Notary;

- The words "Notary Public, State of Texas" around a star of five points; and

- The Notary's commission expiration date.

L.S. The letters "L.S." — abbreviating the Latin term *locus sigilli*, meaning "location of the seal" — appear on many notarial certificates to indicate where the Notary seal should be placed. While an embossing seal may be affixed over these letters, an inking stamp should be imprinted near but not over the letters.

Placement of the Seal Impression. The Notary's official seal impression should be placed near the Notary's signature on the notarial certificate.

Whenever possible — and especially with documents that will be submitted to a public recorder — the Notary should avoid affixing the seal over any text on the document or certificate. Some recorders will reject documents if writing or document text intrudes within the borders the Notary's seal. If there is no room for a seal, the Notary may have no choice but to complete and attach a loose certificate that duplicates the notarial wording on the document. With documents that will *not* be publicly recorded, however, the recipient may allow the Notary to affix the seal over boilerplate text — the standard clauses or sections — as long as the wording within the seal is not obscured.

Fees for Notarial Services

Maximum Fees. The following maximum fees for performing notarial acts are allowed by Texas law: (TGC, Sec. 406.024)

- Acknowledgments — $6. For taking an acknowledgment, the Notary may charge $6 for the first signature on a document, plus $1 for each additional signature on that same document.

- Certified Copies — $6. For certifying a copy, the Notary may charge $6 for each certified copy certificate .

- Certified Copies of Notarial Records — 50¢. For providing a copy of a Notary record — either an entry in the Notary's

49

official journal or any paper in the Notary's office — the Notary may charge 50¢ for each page in addition to the $6 fee for the certificate.

- <u>Depositions — $6 plus 50¢ per 100 words</u>. For swearing a witness to a deposition, including completing the certificate, affixing the seal and other connected business, the fee is $6. For taking the deposition of a witness, the fee is 50¢ for each 100 words.

- <u>Jurats — $6</u>. For executing a jurat on an affidavit or other form of verification upon oath or affirmation, the Notary may charge $6 for each signature.

- <u>Oaths and Affirmations — $6</u>. For administering an oath or affirmation with certificate and seal, the Notary may charge $6.

- <u>Proof of Acknowledgment — $6</u>. For taking a proof of acknowledgment, the Notary may charge $6 for the first signature of each absent principal signer, plus $1 for each additional signature proven.

- <u>Protests — $4</u>. For protesting a bill or note, the fee is $4. For serving a notice of protest, the fee is $1. For protesting in all other cases, the fee is $4. For the certificate and seal to a protest, the fee is $4.

- <u>All Other Notarial Acts — $6</u>. For performing any other notarial act or for completing a certificate and seal not otherwise provided for, the Notary may charge $6.

<u>Travel Fees</u>. Charges for travel by a Notary are not specified by law. Such fees are proper only if Notary and signer agree beforehand on the amount to be charged. The signer must understand that a travel fee is not stipulated in law and is separate from the notarial fees described above.

<u>Option Not to Charge</u>. Notaries are not required to charge for their notarial services. And they may charge any fee less than the statutory maximum.

<u>Overcharging</u>. If a Notary charges more than the legally

prescribed fees, the Notary is liable to the person overcharged for four times the fee unlawfully demanded. (TGC, Secs. 406.024 and 603.010)

In addition, if a Notary charges more than the statutory maximum, his or her commission may be suspended or revoked by the Secretary of State. (TGC, Sec. 406.009)

Fee Book. Notaries must keep a fee book — a record of the fees charged for notarial services — which shall be subject to public inspection at any time. This fee book may be the same as the Notary journal, with the fees charged included with other journal entries. (See "Journal of Notarial Acts," pages 43–46.) (TGC, Sec. 603.006)

Posting of Fees. A Texas Notary is required to post in some conspicuous place in his or her office a table of the fees allowed by law to be charged. (TGC, Sec. 603.008)

Obligation to Itemize. A Notary must itemize or be prepared to itemize in a signed bill the fees he or she charges for services. (TGC, Sec. 603.007)

Disqualifying Interest

Impartiality. Notaries are appointed by the state to be impartial, disinterested witnesses whose screening duties help ensure the integrity of important legal and commercial transactions. Lack of impartiality by a Notary throws doubt on the integrity and lawfulness of any transaction. A Notary must never notarize his or her own signature, or notarize in a transaction in which the Notary has a financial or beneficial interest.

Financial or Beneficial Interest. A Notary should not perform any notarization related to a transaction in which that Notary or the Notary's spouse has a direct financial or beneficial interest. A financial or beneficial interest exists when the Notary or the Notary's spouse is individually named as a principal in a financial transaction or when the Notary receives an advantage, right, privilege, property, or fee valued in excess of the lawfully prescribed notarial fee.

In regard to real estate transactions, a Notary is generally considered to have a disqualifying financial or beneficial interest when that Notary or the Notary's spouse is a grantor or grantee, a mortgagor or mortgagee, a trustor or trustee, a vendor or vendee, a lessor or lessee, or a beneficiary in any way of the transaction.

Employees, Officers and Shareholders. An employee of a corporation may notarize documents in which the corporation has an interest. Also, an officer who is a shareholder in a corporation may notarize documents in which the corporation has an interest — *unless* the corporation has 1,000 or fewer shareholders and the officer owns more than one-tenth of one percent of the issued and outstanding stock. (TCPRC, Sec. 121.002)

Relatives. State officials strongly discourage Notaries from notarizing for persons related by blood or marriage, because of the likelihood for a financial or beneficial interest, whether large or small. This is especially pertinent with spouses, because Texas is a state with community property laws. (NPEM)

Refusal of Services

Legal Request for Services. Notaries must honor all lawful and reasonable requests to notarize, whether or not the person requesting the act is a client or customer of the Notary or the Notary's employer. (TCPRC, Sec. 121.014)

Notaries are appointed by the state of Texas to serve the general public, even when their appointment fee, seal and notarial supplies are paid for by a private employer.

A person's race, gender, religion, nationality, ethnicity, lifestyle or politics is never legitimate cause for refusing to perform a notarial act. As a public servant, a Notary should treat all people fairly and equally.

Reasonable Care

Responsibility. As public servants, Notaries must act responsibly and exercise reasonable care in the performance of their official duties. If a Notary fails to do so, he or she may be subject to a civil suit to recover financial damages caused by the Notary's error or omission.

In general, reasonable care is that degree of concern and attentiveness that a person of normal intelligence and responsibility would exhibit. If a Notary can show to a judge or jury that he or she did everything expected of a reasonable person, the judge or jury is obligated by law to find the Notary blameless and not liable for damages.

Complying with all pertinent laws is the first rule of reasonable care for a Notary. If there are no statutory guidelines in a given instance, the Notary should go to extremes to use common sense and prudence. (See "Steps to Proper Notarization," pages 12–16.)

Unauthorized Practice of Law

Do Not Assist with Legal Matters. A Notary may not give legal advice or accept fees for legal advice. As a ministerial officer, a nonattorney Notary is generally not permitted to assist in drafting, preparing, selecting, completing or explaining a document or transaction. (TGC, Sec. 406.016 and NPEM)

The Notary should not fill in blank spaces in the text of a document for other persons, tell others what documents they need nor how to draft them, nor advise others about the legal sufficiency of a document — and especially not for a fee.

A Notary, of course, may fill in the blanks on the portion of a document containing the notarial wording. And a Notary, as a private individual, may prepare legal documents to which he or she is personally a party; but the Notary may not then notarize his or her signature on those same documents.

Notaries who overstep their authority by advising others on legal matters may have their commissions revoked and may be prosecuted for the unauthorized practice of law.

Do Not Determine Notarial Act. A Notary who is not an attorney may not determine the type of notarial act to perform or decide which certificate to attach. This is beyond the scope of the Notary's expertise and would be considered the unauthorized practice of law. The Notary should only follow instructions provided by the document, its signer, its issuing agency or its receiving agency, or by an attorney. (NPEM)

If a document lacks notarial certificate wording, the Notary must ask the document signer what type of notarization — acknowledgment or jurat — is required. The Notary may then type the appropriate notarial wording on the document or attach a preprinted, loose certificate. If the signer does not know what type of notarization is required, the issuing or receiving agency should be contacted to determine the type of notarization required. This decision is *never* the Notary's to make unless the Notary is also an attorney.

Exceptions. Nonattorney Notaries who are specially trained,

certified or licensed in a particular field (e.g., real estate, insurance, escrow) may advise others about documents in that field, but in no other. In addition, trained paralegals under the supervision of an attorney may advise others about documents in routine legal matters.

Signature by Mark

<u>Mark Serves as Signature</u>. A person who cannot sign his or her name because of illiteracy or a physical disability may instead use a mark — an "X" for example — as a signature, as long as there are witnesses to the making of the mark.

<u>Witnesses for Notarization</u>. For a signature by mark to be notarized, there must be *two* witnesses to the making of the mark. (TCPRC, Sec. 121.011)

Both witnesses should also sign the document, and one witness should write out the marker's name beside the mark. These two witnesses should be in addition to the Notary. It is recommended that a mark also be affixed in the Notary's journal, and that the witnesses also sign the journal.

<u>Notarization Procedures</u>. Because a properly witnessed mark is regarded as a legal signature, no special procedures are required. The marker must be positively identified, as must any other signer, and regular notarial certificates may be used.

Signing for Person Physically Unable to Sign

Effective September 1, 1997, a Texas Notary may sign the name of a person who is physically unable to grip and use a pen. This new procedure will be of particular benefit to suddenly disabled individuals who had not appointed an attorney in fact to sign for them. (TGC, Sec. 406.0165)

Such a proxy signature may only be affixed on a document that is presented for notarization and only if the Notary has been asked to affix such a signature by the disabled individual and if there is a witness present, in addition to the Notary, who has no financial interest in the transaction.

The disabled person may direct the Notary to sign on his or her behalf either orally or through some mechanical or electrical device that both the Notary and witness can clearly understand.

This procedure may only be used with persons who are physically unable to sign. It may not be used with a person who cannot sign because of illiteracy or who prefers to have another sign as a matter of convenience. It may not be used with documents that do not need notarization.

Identification of Signer. Both the disabled signer and the witness must be identified by the Notary either through personal knowledge, a credible identifying witness personally known to the Notary, or through an authorized ID card. Beneath the proxy signature, the Notary must write:

> Signature affixed by Notary in the presence of _____ (name of witness), under Section 406.0165, Government Code.

Validity of Signature. A signature properly made using this procedure is as valid as if a normal signature had been made by the disabled individual.

Certificate. After the Notary affixes a proxy signature and the required short statement on the document, no special notarial certificate is required. As with any signer, the disabled person should be screened for identity, willingness and basic competence. However, the Notary should note the special circumstances in the journal entry.

Notarizing for Minors

Under Age 18. Generally, persons must reach the age of majority before they can handle their own legal affairs and sign documents for themselves. In Texas, the age of majority is 18. Normally, natural guardians (parents) or court-appointed guardians will sign on a minor's behalf. In certain cases, minors may lawfully sign documents and have their signatures notarized — minors engaged in business transactions or children serving as court witnesses, for example.

Include Age Next to Signature. When notarizing for a minor, the Notary should ask the young signer to write his or her age next to the signature on the document and in the journal. This will alert any interested party that the signer is a minor. The Notary is not required to verify the minor signer's age.

Identification. The method for identifying a minor is the same as that for an adult. However, determining the identity of a minor can be a problem, because minors often do not possess acceptable identification documents, such as driver's licenses or passports. If the minor does not have an acceptable ID, then the other methods of identifying signers must be used, either the Notary's personal knowledge of the minor or the oath of a credible identifying witness who can identify the minor. (See "Identifying Document Signers," pages 40–43.)

Authentication

<u>Documents Sent Out of State</u>. Documents notarized in Texas and sent out of state may be required to bear proof that the Notary's signature and stamp are genuine and that the Notary had authority to act at the time of notarization. This process of proving the genuineness of an official signature and stamp is called *authentication* or *legalization*.

In Texas, the proof is in the form of an authenticating certificate attached to the notarized document by the Secretary of State's Notary Public Unit. These authenticating certificates are known by many different names: certificates of official character, certificates of authority, certificates of capacity, certificates of prothonotary and "flags."

The fee for an authenticating certificate is $10 per document (check or money order, payable to "Secretary of State). The certificate may be obtained by mail by writing to: Secretary of State, Notary Public Unit, P.O. Box 12079, Austin, Texas 78711-2079. You may also obtain a certificate in person from: Secretary of State, Notary Public Unit, 1019 Brazos, #214, Austin, Texas.

The notarized document should *not* be forwarded with the request. All that is needed is a written request stating the Notary's name and commission expiration date, along with the fee. It is not the Notary's responsibility to pick up or pay for the certificate of authority.

<u>Documents Sent Out of Country</u>. If a notarized document will be sent out of the United States, a chain-authentication process may be necessary and additional certificates of authority may have to be obtained from the U.S. Department of State and different ministries of a given foreign nation, here and abroad. This chain-certification process can be time-consuming and expensive.

<u>*Apostilles* and the Hague Convention</u>. Fortunately, over 50 nations, including the United States, subscribe to a treaty under auspices of the Hague Conference that simplifies authentication

of notarized documents exchanged between any of these nations. The official name of this treaty, adopted by the Conference on October 5, 1961, is the Hague Convention Abolishing the Requirement of Legalization for Foreign Public Documents. For a list of the subscribing countries, see "Hague Convention Nations," pages 113–115.

Under the Hague Convention, only one authenticating certificate called an *apostille* is necessary to ensure acceptance of a Notary's signature and stamp in these subscribing countries. (*Apostille* means "notation" in French.)

In Texas, *apostilles* are issued by the Secretary of State for a fee of $10 per document. The procedure is the same as for obtaining an ordinary authenticating certificate, except that the country for which the document is destined should also be specified.

Foreign Languages

Non-English Advertising. A nonattorney Notary advertising notarial services in a foreign language must take steps to guard against misinterpretation of his or her function as a Notary. Notaries are required to include in any such foreign language advertisement the following in English and the foreign language: (TGC, Sec. 406.017)

1) The statement: "I am not an attorney licensed to practice law in Texas and may not give legal advice or accept fees for legal services"; and

2) The fees a Notary is allowed to charge.

The above applies to signs and all other forms of written communication (e.g., business cards, yellow page ads).

Furthermore, literal translation of "Notary Public" into Spanish (*Notario Publico* or *Notaria Publica*) is prohibited by law. For violations of foreign-language advertising law, a Notary's commission can be suspended or revoked. (TGC, Sec. 406.017)

Foreign-Language Documents. Ideally, documents in foreign languages should be referred to Texas Notaries who read and write those languages. If not available in the general public, bilingual Notaries may be often found in foreign consulates.

Texas law does not directly address notarizing documents written in a language the Notary cannot read. Although notarizing such documents is not expressly prohibited, there are difficulties and dangers in notarizing any document the Notary cannot understand. The foremost danger is that the document may have been misrepresented to the Notary. The Notary cannot know if the document is false or endorses or promotes a product using the Notary seal and may unknowingly perform an illegal act or facilitate fraud by notarizing it.

If a Notary chooses to notarize a document that he or she cannot read, at the very least the notarial certificate should be in English, or in a language the Notary can read.

Foreign-Language Signers. There should always be direct communication between the Notary and document signer — whether in English or any other language. The Notary should never rely on an intermediary or interpreter to be assured that a signer is willing, competent and understands the transaction, since this third party may have a motive for misrepresenting the circumstances to the Notary and/or the signer.

Immigration

Do Not Give Advice. Nonattorney Notaries may never advise others on the subject of immigration, nor help others prepare immigration documents — and especially not for a fee. Notaries who offer immigration advice to others may be prosecuted for the unauthorized practice of law. (TGC, Sec. 406.016)

Documents. Affidavits are the forms issued or accepted by the U.S. Immigration and Naturalization Service (INS) that most often require notarization, with the Affidavit of Support (I-134/I-864) being perhaps the most common. Non-INS-issued documents are often notarized and submitted in support of an immigration or naturalization petition. These might include translator's declarations, statements from employers and banks, and affidavits of relationship.

If there appears to be no room for the Texas Notary seal on an INS-issued document, federal officials advise that it may be affixed over boilerplate text (standard clauses or sections).

Naturalization Certificates. A Notary may be in violation of federal law if he or she makes a typewritten, photostatic, or any other copy of a certificate of naturalization or notarizes it. (U.S. Penal Code, Sec. 75 and U.S. Code, Title 18, Sec. 137)

Military-Officer Notarizations

May Notarize Worldwide. Certain U.S. military officers may notarize for military personnel and their dependents anywhere in the world. Under statutory authority, the following persons are authorized to act as Notaries:

- Civilian attorneys employed as legal assistance attorneys and licensed to practice law in the United States.

- Judge advocates on active duty or training as reservists on inactive duty.

- All adjutants, assistant adjutants, acting adjutants and personnel adjutants.

- Enlisted paralegals, personnel rank E-4 or higher, on active duty or training on inactive duty.

- Active duty personnel who are commissioned officers or senior noncommissioned officers (rank E-7 or higher) who are stationed at a Geographically Separated Unit (GSU) or location where no authorized Notary official is available, and who are appointed in writing by the unit's servicing general courtmartial convening authority.

Certificate. When signing documents in their official capacity, military-officer Notaries must specify the date and location of the notarization, list their title and office, and use a raised seal or inked stamp citing Title 10 U.S.C. 1044a. (U.S. Code, Title 10, Sections 936, 1044a)

Authentication. Authentication of a military-officer notarization certificate is not required.

Authority to Notarize. It will be presumed that the officer was, in fact, a commissioned officer and that the acknowledger was a member of the military or the spouse of a member of the military on the date of notarization, unless evidence is offered otherwise. In such military-officer notarizations, failure to affix an official seal does not invalidate the acknowledgment or proof. (TCPRC, Sec. 121.001)

Wills

<u>Do Not Offer Advice</u>. Often, people attempt to draw up wills on their own without benefit of legal counsel and then bring these homemade testaments to a Notary to have them "legalized," expecting the Notary to know how to proceed. In advising or assisting such persons, the Notary risks prosecution for the unauthorized practice of law. The Notary's ill-informed advice may do considerable damage to the affairs of the signer and subject the Notary to a civil lawsuit to recover losses.

Wills are highly sensitive documents, the format of which is dictated by strict laws. The slightest deviation from these laws can nullify a will. In some cases, holographic (handwritten) wills have actually been voided by notarization because the document was not entirely in the handwriting of the testator.

<u>Do Not Proceed Without Certificate Wording</u>. A Notary should notarize a document described as a will only if a notarial certificate is provided or stipulated for each signer, and the signers are not asking questions about how to proceed. Any such questions should properly be answered by an attorney.

<u>Living Wills</u>. Documents that are popularly called living wills may be notarized. These are not actually wills at all, but written statements of the signer's wishes concerning medical treatment in the event that person has an illness or injury and is unable to issue instructions on his or her own behalf.

MISCONDUCT, FINES AND PENALTIES

Prohibited Acts

<u>Unauthorized Practice of Law</u>. A Notary may not give legal advice or accept fees for legal advice. As a ministerial officer, the nonattorney Notary is generally not permitted to assist other persons in drafting, preparing, selecting, completing or understanding a document or transaction. (See "Unauthorized Practice of Law," pages 53–54.) (TGC, Sec. 406.016 and NPEM)

<u>Failure to Affix Seal Impression</u>. A Notary must not fail to attach a seal impression to any document he or she notarizes. An instrument missing the official seal will be considered invalid. A Notary may be subject to civil action by aggrieved parties. (TGC, Sec. 406.054 and TCPRC, Sec. 121.014)

Issue Identification. A Notary may not issue identification cards or documents. (TGC, Sec. 406.016)

Notarize Own Signature. Notaries are not permitted to notarize their own signatures. (NPEM)

Notarize Under Another Name. A Notary must sign the name under which he or she was commissioned — the name that appears on the commission paper — to certify notarial acts. No other name may be used. (NPEM)

Certify Copies of Recordable Documents. Texas Notaries may not certify copies of recordable documents. A document does not have to be recorded, but merely recordable for the Notary to be prohibited from making a certified copy. (See "Certified Copies," pages 26–28.) (TGC, Sec. 406.016 and NPEM)

Failure to Require Personal Appearance. A Notary may not notarize any document without the signer being present — personally appearing — before the Notary. (TGC, Sec. 406.009)

Overcharging. A Notary may not charge more than the maximum fees allowed by law. If a Notary charges more than the legally prescribed fees, the Notary may have his or her commission suspended or revoked by the Secretary of State. (TGC, Sec. 406.024 and NPEM)

In addition, the Notary is liable to the person overcharged for four times the fee unlawfully demanded. (TGC, Sec. 603.010)

Translating "Notary Public" into Spanish. Notaries are prohibited from translating the term "Notary Public" into Spanish (*Notario Publico* or *Notaria Publica*). (TGC, Sec. 406.017)

Copy or Notarize Naturalization Certificates. It can be a serious violation of federal law to make a typewritten, photostatic, or any other copy of a certificate of naturalization or notarize it. Severe penalties are prescribed, including imprisonment. (U.S. Penal Code, Sec. 75 and U.S. Code, Title 18, Sec. 137)

Denial, Suspension or Revocation of Commission

Authority of Secretary of State. The Texas Secretary of State may, for good cause, suspend or revoke the commission of a

Notary Public. In such case, the Notary has the right to be given notice, to have a hearing and to appeal. (TGC, Sec. 406.009)

Application Misstatement. The Texas Secretary of State may deny a Notary commission to any applicant who submits an application containing a knowingly made false statement. (TGC, Sec. 406.009)

Conviction of Felony or Crime of Moral Turpitude. A Notary who is convicted of a felony or crime involving moral turpitude may have his or her commission application denied by the Secretary of State. (TGC, Sec. 406.009)

Violation of Notarial Law. A Notary who is convicted of violating a law concerning the regulation or conduct of Notaries in Texas or another state may have his or her commission application denied by the Secretary of State. (TGC, Sec. 406.009)

Similarly, if a Notary receives an administrative, criminal or civil penalty for violation of a Notary rule or law, his or her commission application may be denied. (TGC, Sec. 406.009)

Disposition of Records. If removed from office, the ex-Notary must deliver his or her journal and public papers to the County Clerk in which the Notary resides. (See "Disposition of Notary Records," page 46.) (TGC, Sec. 406.022)

Overcharging. If a Notary charges more than the legally prescribed fees, the Notary's commission may be suspended or revoked by the Secretary of State. (TGC, Sec. 406.024 and NPEM)

In addition, the Notary is liable to the person overcharged for four times the fee unlawfully demanded. (TGC, Sec. 603.010)

Improper Foreign-Language Advertising. A nonattorney Notary who advertises notarial services in a language other than English and who fails to post the required conspicuous notice in both English and in the foreign language (i.e., "I am not an attorney licensed to practice law in Texas and may not give legal advice or accept fees for legal advice.") may have his or her commission suspended or revoked by the Secretary of State. Failure to include in the notice the fees a Notary may charge is also cause for commission suspension or revocation. (TGC, Sec. 406.009 and 406.017)

NOTARY LAWS EXPLAINED

A Notary who literally translates the phrase "Notary Public" into Spanish (*Notario Publico* or *Notaria Publica*) may have his or her commission suspended or revoked. (TGC, Sec. 406.009 and 406.017)

In addition to a violation of any other law, failure to comply with either of the preceding is a deceptive trade practice actionable under Chapter 17, Business and Commerce Code. (TGC, Sec. 406.017)

Failure to Require Personal Appearance. A Notary who performs a notarization when the signer or oath taker does not personally appear before the Notary at the time of notarization may have his or her commission suspended or revoked by the Secretary of State. (TGC, Sec. 406.009)

Neglect of Duty. A Notary who is found guilty of wilful neglect of duty or malfeasance (misconduct) *may* be removed from office. A Notary who is indicted for and convicted of a willful neglect of duty or malfeasance *shall* be removed from office. (TGC, Sec. 406.018)

Failure to Maintain Residency. If a Notary moves his or her residence out of Texas, he or she vacates the office of Notary. Such a move has the same effect as resignation. (TGC, Sec. 406.020)

An ex officio Notary — one who acquires notarial powers because of a particular office or position — who moves permanently from his or her assigned jurisdiction vacates the office of Notary Public. Such a move has the same effect as resignation. (TGC, Sec. 406.021)

Civil Lawsuit

Liable for All Damages. A person injured by the failure, refusal or neglect of a Notary may sue to recover damages. (TCPRC, Sec. 121.014)

As a ministerial official, a Texas Notary is liable for all damages caused by any intentional or unintentional misconduct or neglect. The $10,000 bond offers no protection to the Notary, since the Notary will be required to reimburse the bonding firm for any funds paid out to a victim of the Notary's misconduct. A civil lawsuit against the Notary may seek financial recovery for the full extent of damages. (NPEM)

Notary errors and omissions insurance, on the other hand,

does provide protection for a Notary who is sued for damages resulting from *unintentional* mistakes made while performing notarial acts. Such insurance is optional and is available from many sources. Errors and omissions insurance does *not* cover the Notary for intentional misconduct.

Appeal of Penalty

Hearing. A Notary whose commission has been suspended or revoked by the Secretary of State has rights to notice, hearing, adjudication and appeal. An appeal is to the District Court of Travis County. The Secretary of State has the burden of proof, and the trial is conducted as if there were no previous judgment. (TGC, Sec. 406.009) ■

Test Your Knowledge

Trial Exam

<u>Instructions</u>. This examination is designed to test your knowledge of the basic concepts of notarization.

Work through the exam without looking at the answers, then check your responses and note where you need additional study. Careful review of "Notary Laws Explained" (pages 17–64), the reprinted Notary statutes (pages 71–98), "10 Most-Asked Questions" (pages 7–11) and "Steps to Proper Notarization" (pages 12–16) will produce the answers.

A perfect score on this examination is 100 points. There are:

- 20 true/false questions worth 1 point each
- 5 multiple-choice questions worth 4 points each
- 5 fill-in-the-blank questions worth 4 points each
- 5 essay questions worth 8 points each.

Now, get a separate sheet of paper and a pen or pencil, and get ready to test your knowledge.

<u>Part 1: True/False</u>. For the following statements, answer true or false. Each correct answer is worth 1 point:

1. Notaries may act only in the county where they are commissioned. True or false?

2. The maximum Notary fee for taking the acknowledgment of three signers is $15. True or false?

3. It is a Notary's duty to serve all persons requesting lawful

TEXAS NOTARY LAW PRIMER

notarial acts, even those who are not customers. True or false?

4. Notaries must keep a photocopy of every document notarized. True or false?

5. A deposition is oral testimony that is written down and used as evidence in a court proceeding. True or false?

6. Notaries can withhold their services if they believe a signer is incompetent and unable to understand a document. True or false?

7. It is a Notary's duty to draft powers of attorney, mortgages, and deeds, upon request. True or false?

8. The letters "L.S." stand for the Latin words *locus sigilli*, which mean "location of the seal." True or false?

9. Holographic wills must be notarized to be valid. True or false?

10. A credible witness vouches for the identity of a signer in the Notary's presence and a subscribing witness for the identity of a signer out of the Notary's presence. True or false?

11. Notaries may notarize documents executed by the company that employs them. True or false?

12. A Notary who does not charge fees is not required to keep a journal. True or false?

13. The Notary needn't reimburse the surety company for bond funds paid out to a person financially harmed by the Notary's actions. True or false?

14. A Notary may not investigate whether a signer does indeed have authority to sign as a corporate officer. True or false?

15. A Notary's seal and journal belong to the Notary's employer if the employer paid for them. True or false?

16. An acknowledgment certificate is not to be used for jurats or proofs of execution by a subscribing witness. True or false?

TEST YOUR KNOWLEDGE

17. An affirmation is the legal equivalent of an oath, but has no reference to a Supreme Being. True or false?

18. If presented with a document that does not include notarial wording, the Notary should attach and complete an acknowledgment. True or false?

19. Notaries may not refuse to notarize blank or incomplete documents if they are signed in the Notary's presence. True or false?

20. A Notary may notarize a deed for a spouse. True or false?

Multiple Choice. Choose the one best answer to each question. Each correct answer is worth 4 points.

1. A Notary has a disqualifying interest when acting as...
    a. A legal secretary typing papers under the instruction of an employer-attorney for a client.
    b. A bank employee preparing loan documents.
    c. A real estate agent selling a condominium.

2. To become a Notary, an applicant must...
    a. Have been a state resident for at least one year.
    b. Be at least 18 years old.
    c. Pass an oral exam given by the governor's office.

3. A certificate of authority for a Notary may be obtained...
    a. From the Governor's office or the County Clerk.
    b. From a stationery store or the Notary himself/herself.
    c. From the Secretary of State.

4. "Satisfactory evidence" of identity means reliance on...
    a. ID cards or a credible witness.
    b. ID cards or personal knowledge of identity.
    c. A credible witness or personal knowledge of identity.

5. A Texas Notary may...
    a. Take depositions and affidavits.
    b. Correct obvious errors in the document being notarized.
    c. Certify a copy of a foreign birth certificate.

TEXAS NOTARY LAW PRIMER

Fill in the Blank. Write in the word or phrase that best completes each sentence. Each correct answer is worth 4 points.

1. The Notary and the Notary's _____ are liable for the Notary's neglect or official misconduct.

2. A solemn, spoken pledge that is not an affirmation is called an _____.

3. An acceptable ID card should contain a signature and a _____ of its bearer.

4. A certified copy certifies the _____ of the reproduction.

5. Wills written entirely in the testator's own handwriting are called _____.

Essay. Reply to each question or statement with a short paragraph. Each complete and correct response is worth 8 points.

1. Discuss the distinctions between a Notary bond and Notary errors and omissions insurance.

2. How does a proof of acknowledgment by subscribing witness work?

3. What is an *apostille* and when is it used?

4. Why should a Notary always complete the journal entry before filling out a notarial certificate?

5. Outline the differences between an acknowledgment certificate and a jurat.

Test Answers

True/False. 1. F; 2. F; 3. T; 4. F; 5. T; 6. T; 7. F; 8. T; 9. F; 10. T; 11. T; 12. F; 13. F; 14. F; 15. F; 16. T; 17. T; 18. F; 19. F; 20. F

Multiple Choice. 1. c; 2. b; 3. c; 4. a; 5. a

Fill In The Blank. 1. Surety; 2. Oath; 3. Photograph;

TEST YOUR KNOWLEDGE

4. Accuracy; 5. Holographic

Essay. Responses should include the basic information in the paragraphs below:

1. A Notary bond, obtained through a state-licensed surety company, provides protection for the public in case of the Notary's negligence or intentional misconduct. Up to the cash limit of the bond, the surety agrees to pay damages to anyone who suffers a loss because of the Notary's actions; the Notary, however, must reimburse the surety. Notary errors and omissions insurance, also purchased from a state-licensed company, protects the Notary in case of an unintentional error, up to the policy limit. The Notary does not reimburse the insurance company. A bond is required by law; errors and omissions insurance is not.

2. A proof of acknowledgment in lieu of an acknowledgment is sometimes used when a document's principal signer is unavailable to appear before a Notary. In most such cases, the principal will be out of town, out of state or even out of the country. A subscribing witness who has either seen the principal sign the document or taken the principal's acknowledgment of the signature may present this document to a Notary on the principal's behalf. The witness must sign (subscribe) the document in addition to the principal. The witness, who must be personally known to the Notary, is given an oath by the Notary. A person who is a grantee or beneficiary of a document should not serve as a subscribing witness.

3. An *apostille* is a certificate authenticating the signature and seal of a Notary. It is issued under provisions of an international treaty, signed by more than 50 nations, called the Hague Convention Abolishing the Requirement of Legalization for Foreign Public Documents. For notarized documents exchanged between the subscribing nations, this treaty streamlines the time-consuming authentication process known as "chain certification" by requiring only one authenticating certificate, the *apostille* (French for "notation"). *Apostilles* for Texas Notaries are issued by the Secretary of State in Austin.

4. Filling out a journal entry before completing a notarial certificate prevents a signer from grabbing the document and leaving before an important record of the notarization is made in the journal.

5. An acknowledgment certificate certifies that the signer of the document personally appeared before the Notary on the date and in the county indicated. It also certifies that the signer's identity was satisfactorily proven to the Notary and that the signer acknowledged having signed freely. A jurat certifies that the person signing the document did so in the Notary's presence, that the person appeared before the Notary on the date and in the county indicated, and that the Notary administered an oath or affirmation to the signer. For a jurat, it is also advisable to positively identify the signer.

Tally Your Score

After checking your answers, add up your score. Then look at the grading scale below to determine how you stand:

- 90–100: Excellent!
- 80–89: Good, but some review needed.
- 70–79: Fair. Reread the parts of the *Primer* covering the answers you missed.
- Below 70: Below par. Study the laws thoroughly again. ■

Texas Laws Pertaining to Notaries Public

Reprinted on the following pages are the *Notary Public Education Materials* issued to newly commissioned Notaries by the Secretary of State. Also reprinted are the pertinent parts of Texas statutes affecting Notaries and notarial acts. These laws include legislation in effect starting September 1, 1997.

NOTARY PUBLIC EDUCATION MATERIALS

**Secretary of State
Notary Public Unit
P.O. Box 12079
Austin, TX 78711-2079**

Foreword

The following educational materials are provided to you in accordance with Tex. Gov't Code Ann. § 406.008.

This information should be kept for reference throughout your four (4) year term. Please read through this information at least once before you begin to notarize in order to familiarize yourself with the responsibilities of your office.

THE STATUTES REFERRED TO IN THESE MATERIALS ARE SUBJECT TO LEGISLATIVE CHANGE. The Secretary of State will provide a copy of these changes only upon request. Contact the Secretary of State, Notary Public Unit, P.O. Box 13375, Austin, Texas 78711-3375 or call (512) 463-5705 following each legislative session.

The Secretary of State's office would like to thank the Texas Young Lawyers Association for permitting us to use excerpts from their former publication, *Texas Notary Public Handbook*.

TABLE OF CONTENTS*

Introduction..Page 72
Statutes
   Record Book and Public Records ....Page 73
   Notary Seal ....Page 73
   Change of Address...Page 74
   Unauthorized Practice of law ....Page 74
   Revocation or Suspension of Commission by
      the Secretary of State ....Page 75
   Fees Posted...Page 75
   Fee Book ....Page 75
   To Itemize Costs..Page 75
   Fees..Page 76
Questions Frequently Asked ....Page 76
List of Prohibited Acts ....Page 78
Notarial Definitions...Page 79
Sample Forms
   Acknowledgments ....Page 80
   Jurat...Page 81
   Verifications ....Page 81
   Oath or Affirmation ....Page 82
   Statements of Officer ....Page 82
   Deposition ....Page 83
   Protests ....Page 83
   Certified Copy of a Non-Recordable Document ....Page 84

INTRODUCTION

    A Notary Public is a public servant with statewide jurisdiction who is authorized to take acknowledgments, protest instruments permitted by law to be protested (primarily negotiable instruments and bills and notes), administer oaths, take depositions, and certify copies of documents not recordable in the public records.

    A Notary Public is, in the true sense of the word, "a public servant" and "an officer of the State of Texas", conveniently located in the community so that he/she may be of service to the public. Each Notary Public takes an official oath of office to faithfully perform the duties of the office, and to insure such performance is required to post a $10,000.00 bond with the Secretary of State.

    The primary duty of a Notary Public is to show a disinterested party (the Notary Public) has admonished the signer of an instrument as to the importance of such a document, and the signer of such document has declared that his/her identity, his/her signature and his/her reasons for signing such instrument are genuine. The signature and seal of a Notary Public do not prove these facts conclusively, but do provide prima facie proof of them, and allow persons in trade and commerce to rely upon the truth and veracity of the Notary Public as a third party who has no personal interest in the transaction.

    A Notary Public is personally liable for negligence or fraud in the

---

* Page numbers refer to the pages in this *Primer*. Page numbers will differ in the actual *Notary Public Education Materials*.

performance of the duties of the office. The bond is to insure that the person injured can recover at least $10,000.00, but this does not protect the Notary Public from personal liability for the full extent of damages caused by a breach of official duty. In addition to civil liability, Notaries Public may be subject to criminal prosecution and the revocation or suspension of their Notary Public commission by the Secretary of State's office.

The Secretary of State's office may revoke or suspend the Commission of any Notary Public for good cause subject to Tex. Gov't Code Ann. § 406.009 and the notary public rules. A high standard of conduct should always be maintained by a Notary Public.

Statutes
RECORD BOOK AND PUBLIC RECORDS

Tex. Gov't Code Ann. § 406.014 requires, that a Notary Public maintain a record book. This record book must be maintained whether or not any fees are charged for your notary public services.

> A notary public other than a court clerk notarizing instruments for the court shall keep in a book a record of: (1) the date of each instrument notarized; (2) the date of the notarization; (3) the name of the signer, grantor, or maker; (4) the signer's, grantor's, or maker's residence or alleged residence; (5) whether the signer, grantor, or maker is personally known by the notary public, was identified by an identification card issued by a governmental agency or a passport issued by the United States, or was introduced to the notary public and, if introduced, the name and residence or alleged residence of the individual introducing the signer, grantor, or maker; (6) if the instrument is proved by a witness, the residence of the witness, whether the witness is personally known by the notary public or was introduced to the notary public and, if introduced, the name and residence of the individual introducing the witness; (7) the name and residence of the grantee; (8) if land is conveyed or charged by the instrument, the name and residence of the original grantee and the county where the land is located; and (9) a brief description of the instrument. Entries in the notary's book are public information. A notary public shall, on payment of all fees, provide a certified copy of any record in the notary public's office to any person requesting the copy.

NOTARY SEAL

Tex. Gov't Code Ann. § 406.013 requires a Notary Public to use a seal of office to authenticate all his/her acts. A printed seal does not mean a hand drawn seal.

> (a) A notary public shall provide a seal of office that clearly shows, when embossed, stamped, or printed on a document, the words, "Notary Public, State of Texas" around a star of five points, the notary public's name, and the date the notary public's commission expires. The notary public shall authenticate all his official acts with the seal of office.
>
> (b) The seal may be a circular form not more than two inches in

diameter or a rectangular form not more than one inch in width and 2-1/2 inches in length. The seal must have a serrated or milled edge border.

(c) The seal must be affixed by a seal press or stamp that embosses or prints a seal that legibly reproduces the required elements of the seal under photographic methods. An indelible ink pad must be used for affixing by a stamp the impression on an instrument to authenticate the notary public's official act.

CHANGE OF ADDRESS

Tex. Gov't Code Ann. § 406.019 requires a Notary Public to notify the Secretary of State of any change of address within ten (10) days. You may fill out a *Notary Public Change of Address* form or send a letter with your name, social security number, old address, and new address to: Secretary of State, Notary Public Unit, P.O. Box 13375, Austin, Texas 78711-3375.

UNAUTHORIZED PRACTICE OF LAW

Tex. Gov't Code Ann. § 406.017 requires any Notary Public that is not an attorney and advertises in a language other than English to state that they are not an attorney. This section also prohibits the use of "Notario Publico".

In Mexico, a Notary Public must be a lawyer and must have earned at least a bachelor's degree in law. To avoid deception by such persons and to dispel erroneous assumptions, the Texas Legislature enacted Section 406.017 to prescribe special provisions applicable to advertisements by a Notary Public in languages other than English.

(a) A notary public who is not an attorney who advertises the services of a notary public in a language other than English, whether by signs, pamphlets, stationery or other written communication or by radio or television, shall post or otherwise include with the advertisement a notice that the notary public is not an attorney.

(b) The notice must be in English and in the language of the advertisement and in letters of a conspicuous size. If the advertisement is by radio or television, the statement may be modified, but must include substantially the same message. The notice must include the fees that a Notary Public may charge and the following statement:

"I AM NOT AN ATTORNEY LICENSED TO PRACTICE LAW IN TEXAS AND MAY NOT GIVE LEGAL ADVICE OR ACCEPT FEES FOR LEGAL ADVICE."

(c) Literal translation of the phrase "Notary Public" into Spanish is prohibited. In this subsection, "literal translation" means the translation of a word or phrase without regard to the true meaning of the word or phrase in the language that is being translated.

(d) Failure to comply with this section is, in addition to a violation of any other applicable law of this state, a deceptive trade practice actionable under Chapter 17, Business & Commerce Code.

REVOCATION OR SUSPENSION OF COMMISSION BY THE SECRETARY OF STATE

Tex. Gov't Code Ann. § 406.009 gives the Secretary of State the authority to reject an application, or suspend or revoke the commission of any Notary Public for "good cause".

(a) The secretary of state may, for good cause, reject an application or suspend or revoke the commission of a notary public.

(b) An action by the secretary of state under this section is subject to the rights of notice, hearing, adjudication, and appeal.

(c) An appeal under this section is to the district court of Travis County. The secretary of state has the burden of proof, and the trial is conducted de novo.

(d) In this section, "good cause" includes:
(1) a final conviction for a crime involving moral turpitude;
(2) a false statement knowingly made in an application;
(3) the failure to comply with Section 406.017;
(4) a final conviction for a violation of a law concerning the regulation of the conduct of notaries public in this or another state;
(5) the imposition on the notary public of an administrative, criminal, or civil penalty for a violation of a law or rule prescribing the duties of a notary public; or
(6) performing any notarization when the person for whom the notarization is performed did not personally appear before the notary at the time the notarization is executed.

FEES POSTED

Tex. Gov't Code Ann. § 603.008 (Vernon Supp. 1994) requires that a Notary Public keep the fees posted that they are authorized by law to charge.

A county judge, clerk of the district or county court, sheriff, justice of the peace, constable, or notary public shall keep posted at all times in a conspicuous place in the respective offices a complete list of fees the person may charge by law.

FEE BOOK

Tex. Gov't Code Ann. § 603.006 (Vernon Supp. 1994) requires a Notary Public that charges a fee for his/her services to keep a fee book.

An officer who by law may charge a fee for a service shall keep a fee book and shall enter therein all fees charged for services rendered.

TO ITEMIZE COSTS

Tex. Gov't Code Ann. § 603.007 (Vernon Supp. 1994) states that a Notary Public must itemize or be prepared to itemize the fees he/she charges for performing notarial services.

A fee under this chapter is not payable to a person until a clerk or officer produces, or is ready to produce, a bill in writing containing the details of the fee to the person who owes the fee. The bill must be signed by the clerk or officer to whom the fee is due or who charges the fee or by the successor in office or legal representative of the clerk or officer.

FEES

Tex. Gov't Code Ann. § 406.024 sets out the maximum fees a Notary Public, or its employer, may charge for their notary public services. A Notary Public that charges more than the maximum set out below subjects himself/herself to possible criminal prosecution and suspension or revocation of his/her notary public commission by the Secretary of State's office.

For the exact wording of the fee schedule please refer to the Government Code.

Notaries Public may charge the following fees:

Protesting a bill or note for non-acceptance or
   non-payment, register and seal $4.00
Each notice of protest 1.00
Protesting in all cases 4.00
Certificate and seal to such protest 4.00
Taking the acknowledgment or proof of any deed or other instrument
   in writing, for registration, including certificate and seal:
   (1) for the first signature 6.00
   (2) for each additional signature 1.00
Administering an oath or affirmation with certificate and seal 6.00
All certificates under seal not otherwise provided for 6.00
Copies of all records and papers in their office, for each page 50
All notarial acts not provided for 6.00
Taking the depositions of witnesses, for each 100 words 50
Swearing a witness to depositions, making certificate therefor with seal,
   and all other business connected with taking such deposition 6.00

Questions Frequently Asked

The following section consists of questions Notaries Public often have about their office. If you have any questions about notarizing a document you should contact the maker of the document, the Notary Public Unit of the Secretary of State's office, or an attorney.

1. May I notarize my spouse's signature?
2. May I notarize for my spouse's business?
3. May I notarize for my relatives? There is no statute that directly answers these questions. The basic rules are "the act of taking and certifying acknowledgments cannot be performed by a notary public financially or beneficially interested in the transaction", *Creosoted Wood Block Paving Co. v. McKay*, (Civ. App. 1919) 211 S.W. 822, and "one who is party to an instrument, no matter how small or nominal is his interest therein, cannot act as notary public with reference thereto", *Morris v. Dunn*, (Civ. App. 1942) 164 S.W.2d 562. Better practice requires the use of a disinterested Notary Public, so the best answer to each of the questions above is "NO". This is

particularly true with spouses where it appears that either the husband or wife would always have some interest because of Texas community property laws. Alone, none of the above constitutes a valid complaint against a Notary Public which the Secretary of State's office would pursue.

4. May I alter or change the instrument I notarize? To answer this question, a distinction must be made between the instrument and the acknowledgment. A Notary Public is not authorized to change, alter or draft any instrument. However, a Notary Public may correct the certificate of acknowledgment to reflect the proper facts.

For example, if an acknowledgment is taken in Webb County and the certificate shows Marion County, the certificate may be corrected as follows:

> The State of Texas
> County of ~~Marion~~ Webb
> Before me _____ (Notary Public's name), A Notary Public, on this day personally... etc.

5. May I perform notarial acts in other counties? Yes. Jurisdiction to perform notarial acts is co-extensive with the boundaries of the State of Texas.

6. May I perform functions other than those outlined in Tex. Gov't Code § 406.016, and may I charge fees in excess of those authorized in Tex. Gov't Code § 406.024? No. Notary Public functions are statutorily stated and should be provided in accordance with the law prescribed. A Notary Public may not deviate from the prescribed fees for performance of notarial acts.

7. What if there is a difference between the date the instrument is signed and the date the acknowledgment is actually taken? To answer this question, an example is given. If an instrument ends with the wording: *"Signed and executed at Tyler, Smith County, Texas this 25th day of October, 1993,"* and the party whose name appears on such instrument appears before the Notary Public on October 27, 1993, the Notary Public would fill in the acknowledgment with the true and correct date of the appearance before the Notary Public.

8. May I take an acknowledgment on the telephone? No. A Notary Public may not perform by telephone those notarial acts which require a personal appearance.

9. May I change my name from the name shown on my notary public commission? Yes. A Notary Public may change the name on their commission by sending the Secretary of State a name change application, your current certificate of commission, a rider or endorsement from the insurance agency or surety, and a $20.00 filing fee. The above four elements must be sent in at the same time. For an instruction sheet, please contact the Notary Public Unit at 512-463-5705.

10. May I make a certified copy of a birth certificate? No. A birth certificate is a recordable document. However, a Notary Public now has the authority to make certified copies of documents **not** recordable in the public records. This provision was enacted in order to deter fraud and hand-copying mistakes. Two key words a Notary Public can use in determining whether or not they can make a certified copy of a document are "Filed" or "Recorded". If a Notary Public is brought a document which contains either one of these words, the Notary Public may not supply the person with a certified copy. The document need not be recorded, but merely recordable, for the Notary Public to be unable to make a certified copy. The person must obtain a certified copy from the custodian of the record: county clerk, registrar, Secretary of State.

When making certified copies, the Notary Public must be brought the original document. He/she will then make two (2) photocopies, one of which the Notary Public will retain for his/her journal. The types of documents a Notary Public may make certified copies of would include letters or in-house business documents. The Notary Public **may not** make certified copies of birth certificates, death certificates, Deeds of Trust, liens, etc. THESE ARE ALL RECORDABLE DOCUMENTS.

11. May a notary public determine which type of notarial certificate should be attached to a document? No. A Notary Public who is not an attorney should only complete a notarial certificate which is already on the document or type a certificate of the maker's choosing. **If a Notary Public is brought a document without a certificate and decides which certificate to attach, that Notary Public would be "practicing law".** Therefore, never decide which certificate should be used — leave that up to the maker of the document.

12. Should a notary public rely only on a credit card in determining the identification of a signer? No. If the signer is not personally known by the Notary Public or identified by a credible witness, the Notary Public **must** use an identification card issued by a governmental agency or a passport issued by the United States to identify the signer.

Prohibited Acts

THE SECTION BELOW PROVIDES A NOTARY PUBLIC WITH A LIST OF PROHIBITED ACTS HE/SHE MAY NOT DO IN CARRYING OUT THEIR OFFICE. IF THE NOTARY PUBLIC PERFORMS ANY OF THE FOLLOWING, HE/SHE MAY BE SUBJECTING THEMSELVES TO POSSIBLE CRIMINAL PROSECUTION, CIVIL LIABILITY, AND THE REVOCATION OR SUSPENSION OF HIS/HER NOTARY PUBLIC COMMISSION.

A Notary Public may not:

1. perform acts which constitute the practice of law, the performance thereof being restricted to licensed attorneys at law.
2. prepare, draft, select, or give advice concerning legal documents.
3. translate the term "Notary Public" in Spanish (Notario Publico).
4. overcharge for his/her services.
5. notarize a document without the signer being in his/her presence.

6. notarize his/her own signature.
7. issue identification cards.
8. sign a document under any other name than the one under which he/she was commissioned.
9. fail to attach his/her seal to any document he/she notarizes.
10 certify copies of documents recordable in the public records.

Notarial Definitions

Acknowledgment: A formal declaration before an authorized official, by the person who executed the instrument, that it is his/her free act and deed. The certificate of the officer on such instrument that it has been so acknowledged.

Affidavit: A written or printed declaration or statement of facts, made voluntarily, confirmed by the oath or affirmation of the party making it, and taken before a Notary Public or other officer having authority to administer such oath. It is made either with or without notice to adverse parties thereto.

Affirmation: The act of affirming the truth of a document, not an oath. "I solemnly affirm and declare the foregoing to be a true statement..." Note that an affidavit may appear in two forms: a sworn affidavit with oath, or an affirmed affidavit with affirmation. Each has the same legal import.

Jurat: The clause written at the foot of an affidavit or document stating when, where and before whom such affidavit was sworn or affirmed. The expiration date of the Notary Public's Commission is commonly included.

Oath: An external pledge or affirmation, made in verification of statements made or to be made, coupled with an appeal to a sacred or venerated object, in evidence of the seriousness and reverent state of mind of the party; an invocation to a supreme being to witness the words of the party and to visit him with punishment if they be false.

Protest: A statement issued by a Notary Public that a certain bill or note was presented for payment or acceptance, and such payment or acceptance was refused. The Notary Public attests that the refuser shall be liable for any losses arising from the dishonor of the document.

Verification: The ascertaining of an allegation to be true; the acceptance of the Notary that the person appearing before him/her has been properly identified as being the person purported to be; to make sure of proper procedure and verify same; to give a verification over his/her official signature and seal where necessary to the transaction of the business.

SAMPLE FORMS

In the following examples, a personalized seal includes the words "Notary Public, State of Texas" around a star of five points, the Notary Public's name, and the date the Notary Public's commission expires.

TEXAS NOTARY LAW PRIMER

ACKNOWLEDGMENTS

I. Ordinary Certificate

State of Texas
County of _____,
Before me, _____ (the notary public's name), on this day personally appeared _____, known to me (or proved to me on the oath of _____ or through _____ [description of identity card or other document]) to be the person whose name is subscribed to the foregoing instrument and acknowledged to me that he executed the same for the purposes and consideration therein expressed.

Given under my hand and seal of office this _____ day of _____, _____ (year).

(PERSONALIZED SEAL)   Notary Public's Signature

II. Short Forms

A. For a natural person acting in his/her own right:

State of Texas
County of _____
This instrument was acknowledged before me on _____ (date) by _____ (name of person or persons acknowledging).

(PERSONALIZED SEAL)   Notary Public's Signature

B. For a natural person as principal acting by attorney-in-fact:

State of Texas
County of _____
This instrument was acknowledged before me on _____ (date) by _____ (name of attorney in fact) as attorney in fact on behalf of _____ (name of principal).

(PERSONALIZED SEAL)   Notary Public's Signature

C. For a partnership acting by one or more partners:

State of Texas
County of _____
This instrument was acknowledged before me on _____ (date) by _____ (name of acknowledging partner or partners), partner(s) on behalf of _____ (name of partnership), a partnership.

(PERSONALIZED SEAL)   Notary Public's Signature

D. For a corporation:

State of Texas
County of _____
This instrument was acknowledged before me on _____ (date) by _____ (name of officer), _____ (title of officer) of _____ (name of corporation acknowledging), a _____ (state of incorporation) corporation, on behalf of said corporation.

(PERSONALIZED SEAL)   Notary Public's Signature

E. For a public officer, trustee, executor, administrator, guardian, or other representative:

State of Texas
County of _____
This instrument was acknowledged before me on _____ (date) by _____ (name of representative) as _____ (title of representative) of _____ (name of entity or person represented).

(PERSONALIZED SEAL)   Notary Public's Signature

Jurat

State of Texas
County of _____
Sworn to and subscribed before me on the _____ day of _____, _____ (year).

(PERSONALIZED SEAL)   Notary Public's Signature

Verifications

Form 1:

State of Texas
County of _____
_____, personally appeared before me, and being first duly sworn declared that, he/she signed this application in the capacity designated, if any, and further states that he/she has read the above application and the statements therein contained are true.

(PERSONALIZED SEAL)   Notary Public's Signature

Form 2:

State of Texas
County of _____
Before me, a notary public, on this day personally appeared

TEXAS NOTARY LAW PRIMER

_____, known to me to be the person whose name is subscribed to the foregoing document and, being by me first duly sworn, declared that the statements therein contained are true and correct.

(PERSONALIZED SEAL)   Notary Public's Signature

Oath or Affirmation

State of Texas
County of _____
I, _____ (affiant), do solemnly swear (or affirm), that I will faithfully execute the duties of the office of _____ of the State of Texas, and will to the best of my ability preserve, protect, and defend the laws of the United States and of this State, so help me God.

                                                    Signature of Affiant
Sworn to and subscribed before me by _____ (affiant) on this _____ day of _____, _____ (year).

(PERSONALIZED SEAL)   Notary Public's Signature

Statement of Elected Officer

State of Texas
County of _____
I, _____ (name of affiant), do solemnly swear (or affirm), that I have not directly or indirectly paid, offered, promised to pay, contributed, or promised to contribute any money or thing of value, or promised a public office or employment for the giving or withholding of a vote at the election at which I was elected so help me God.
_____ Signature of Affiant
Sworn to and subscribed before me by _____ (affiant) on this _____ day of _____, _____ (year).

(PERSONALIZED SEAL)   Notary Public's Signature

Statement of Appointed Officer

State of Texas
County of _____
I, _____ (name of affiant), do solemnly swear (or affirm), that I have not directly or indirectly paid, offered, promised to pay, contributed, or promised to contribute any money or thing of value, or promised a public office or employment, as a reward to secure my appointment or confirmation thereof, so help me God.
_____ Signature of Affiant
Sworn to and subscribed before me by _____ (affiant) on this _____ day of _____, _____ (year).

(PERSONALIZED SEAL)   Notary Public's Signature

TEXAS LAWS PERTAINING TO NOTARIES PUBLIC

Depositions

Form 1: Certificate To Deposition — Written Questions

The State of Texas
County of _____

_____ (Plaintiff)) In the _____ Court
v.) of _____ County, Texas
_____ (Defendant)) Cause No. _____

I hereby certify that the foregoing answers of _____, the witness forenamed, were signed and sworn to before me on _____ (date), by said witness.

Form 2: Certificate To Deposition — Oral Questions

The State of Texas
County of _____

_____ (Plaintiff)) In the _____ Court
v.) of _____ County, Texas
_____ (Defendant)) Cause No. _____

I, _____ (Notary Public's name), Notary Public in _____ County, Texas, do hereby certify that the said witness _____ (name) was first sworn to testify the truth and nothing but the truth; that he/she was then carefully examined; that his/her testimony which is above given was by me reduced to writing (or typewriting) (or to writing or typewriting by _____ (name), a person under my personal supervision; or by the deponent himself/herself in my presence) and by no other person, and that after it had been so reduced to writing (or typewriting) subscribed by the deponent before me all on _____ day of _____, _____ (year).

_____
(PERSONALIZED SEAL)   Notary Public's Signature

Protests

(Insert bill or note or copy thereof)

United States of America
State of Texas
County of _____
Be it known that on the _____ day of _____, _____ (year), at the request of _____ (name), of _____, I _____ (Notary Public's name), a Notary Public duly commissioned and sworn, residing in _____ County, Texas, did present the original _____ (instrument), hereto attached, for $_____, with accrued interest thereon of $_____, dated _____, and demanded payment (or acceptance) thereof which was refused.
Whereupon I, at the request of the aforesaid _____, did

protest, and by these presents do protest, as well against the drawer, maker, endorsers, and acceptors of said instruments as against all others whom it may concern, for exchange, costs, charges, damages, and interest already incurred and hereinafter to be incurred by reason of non-payment thereof. I further certify that on _____ (date), notice in writing of the foregoing presentment, demand, refusal and protest was given by _____ (persons and status) by depositing notices thereof in the post office at _____, Texas, postage paid, directed as follows: _____. I further certify that notices were left as follows:
Notice left for _____ at _____
Notice left for _____ at _____
Each of the named places the reputed place of residence of the person for whom the notice was left.

    In testimony whereof I have hereunto set my hand and affixed my seal of office at _____ Texas, on _____ day of _____, _____ (year).

                                                             _____
(PERSONALIZED SEAL)   Notary Public's Signature

(List fees and expenses to include postage)

Certified Copy of a Non-Recordable Document

State of Texas
County of _____
On this _____ day of _____, _____ (year), I certify that the preceding or attached document, and the duplicate retained by me as a notarial record, are true, exact, complete, and unaltered photocopies made by me of _____ (description of document), presented to me by the document's custodian, _____, (*held in my custody as a notarial record) and that, to the best of my knowledge, the photocopied document is neither a public record nor a publicly recordable document, certified copies of which are available from an official source other than a notary.

                                                    _____
(PERSONALIZED SEAL)   Notary Public's Signature

    *This phrase would be inserted and the preceding phrase, "presented to me by the document's custodian", would be deleted in the event a person was requesting a certified copy of the Notary Public's journal.

PERTINENT STATUTES GOVERNING TEXAS NOTARIES

Texas Government Code
                        Title 4. Executive Branch
                      Subtitle A. Executive Officers
          Chapter 406. Notary Public; Commissioner of Deeds
                    Subchapter A. Notary Public

Sec. 406.001. Appointments
Sec. 406.002. Term
Sec. 406.003. Jurisdiction
Sec. 406.004. Eligibility
Sec. 406.005. Appointment Procedure — Statement
Sec. 406.006. Qualification
Sec. 406.007. Fees Paid to Secretary of State
Sec. 406.008. Commission; Notary Materials
Sec. 406.009. Rejection of Appointment; Suspension or Revocation of Commission
Sec. 406.010. Bond; Oath
Sec. 406.011. Reappointment
Sec. 406.012. Inspection of records
Sec. 406.013. Seal
Sec. 406.014. Notary Records
Sec. 406.015. Copies Certified by County Clerk
Sec. 406.016. Authority
Sec. 406.0165. Signing Document for Individual with Disability
Sec. 406.017. Representation as Attorney
Sec. 406.018. Removal from Office
Sec. 406.019. Change of Address
Sec. 406.020. Removal from State
Sec. 406.021. Removal from Precinct
Sec. 406.022. Effect of Vacancy
Sec. 406.023. Administration and Enforcement
Sec. 406.024. Fees Charged by Notary Public

Subchapter B. Commissioner of Deeds

Sec. 406.051. Appointment
Sec. 406.052. Term
Sec. 406.053. Oath
Sec. 406.054. Seal
Sec. 406.055. Authority

Subchapter A. Notary Public

Sec. 406.001. Appointments. The secretary of state may appoint a notary public at any time. (1987, ch. 146, sec. 1)

Sec. 406.002. Term. The term of a notary public expires four years after the date the notary qualifies. (1987, ch. 147, sec. 1)

Sec. 406.003. Jurisdiction. A notary public has statewide jurisdiction. (1987, ch. 147, sec. 1)

Sec. 406.004. Eligibility. Each person appointed and commissioned as a notary public shall be at least 18 years of age and a resident of the State of Texas and must not have been convicted of a felony or crime involving moral turpitude. (1987, ch. 147, sec. 1)

Sec. 406.005. Appointment Procedure — Statement. (a) Each person to be appointed a notary public shall submit an application to the secretary of state on a form prescribed by the secretary of state. The application must satisfy the secretary of state that the applicant is qualified. The application must state:

(1) the applicant's name to be used in acting as a notary public;

(2) the applicant's post office address;
(3) the applicant's county of residence;
(4) the applicant's date of birth;
(5) the applicant's driver's license number or the number of other official state-issued identification; and
(6) the applicant's social security number.

(b) The applicant shall also execute the statement of officers as required by Section 1, Article XVI, Texas Constitution.

(c) The statement shall be signed and sworn to or affirmed by the applicant in the presence of a notary public or other person authorized to administer oaths in this state. (1987, ch. 147, sec. 1; 1995, ch. 719, sec. 2)

Sec. 406.006. Qualification. An individual qualifies by:
(1) properly completing the application form;
(2) executing the statement;
(3) providing the bond;
(4) paying the required filing fees; and
(5) meeting the eligibility requirements. (1987, ch. 147, sec. 1; 1989, ch. 406, sec. 1; 1995, ch. 719, sec. 3)

Sec. 406.007. Fees Paid to Secretary of State. (a) The applicant must submit to the secretary of state:
(1) a fee of $10 for approving and filing the bond of the notary public; and
(2) a fee of $1 to be appropriated to and used by the secretary of state only for hiring an investigator and for preparing and distributing the materials required to be distributed under Section 406.008.

(b) The secretary of state shall charge for use of the state a fee of $10 for a notary public commission. The applicant must pay the fee in advance to the secretary of state. (1987, ch. 147, sec. 1; 1989, ch. 4, sec. 2.14)

Sec. 406.008. Commission; Notary Materials. (a) Immediately after the qualification of a notary public, the secretary of state shall send notice of appointment along with a commission to the notary public. The commission is effective as of the date of qualification.

(b) When the commission is issued, the secretary of state shall supply the notary public with:
(1) materials outlining the powers and duties of the office;
(2) a list of prohibited acts; and
(3) sample forms for an acknowledgment, jurat, and verification and for the administering of an oath, protest, and deposition.

(c) Repealed by Acts 1995, 74th Leg., ch. 719, sec. 10, eff. Jan. 1, 1996. (1987, ch. 147, sec. 1; 1995, ch. 719, secs. 4, 10)

Sec. 406.009. Rejection of Appointment; Suspension or Revocation of Commission. (a) The secretary of state may, for good cause, reject an application or suspend or revoke the commission of a notary public.

(b) An action by the secretary of state under this section is subject to the rights of notice, hearing, adjudication, and appeal.

(c) An appeal under this section is to the district court of Travis County. The secretary of state has the burden of proof, and the trial is conducted de novo.

(d) In this section "good cause" includes:
(1) a final conviction for a crime involving moral turpitude;
(2) a false statement knowingly made in an application;

(3) the failure to comply with Section 406.017;

(4) a final conviction for a violation of a law concerning the regulation of the conduct of notaries public in this or another state;

(5) the imposition on the notary public of an administrative, criminal, or civil penalty for a violation of a law or rule prescribing the duties of a notary public; or

(6) performing any notarization when the person for whom the notarization is performed did not personally appear before the notary at the time the notarization was executed.

(e) The dismissal and discharge of proceedings under either the misdemeanor adult probation and supervision law or the adult probation, parole, and mandatory supervision law shall not be considered a conviction for the purposes of determining good cause. (1987, ch. 147, sec. 1; 1989, ch. 4, sec. 2.15; 1995, ch. 719, secs. 5, 8)

Sec. 406.010. Bond; Oath. (a) Each person to be appointed a notary public shall, before entering the official duties of office, execute a bond in the amount of $10,000 with a solvent surety company authorized to do business in this state as a surety. The bond must be approved by the secretary of state, payable to the governor, and conditioned on the faithful performance of the duties of office. The secretary of state has the authority to accept an electronic filing of the notary public bond if an agreement has been made with the surety company.

(b) The notary bond shall be deposited in the office of the secretary of state, is not void on first recovery, and may be sued on in the name of the injured party from time to time until the whole amount of the bond is recovered.

(c) A notary public, before entering on the duties of office, shall take the official oath required by Section 1, Article XVI, Texas Constitution.

(d) The oath shall be signed and sworn to or affirmed by the notary public in the presence of a notary public or other person authorized to administer oaths in this state. A notary public cannot execute his or her own oath of office.

(e) The secretary of state shall provide an oath of office form along with the commission and educational materials. (1987, ch. 147, sec. 1; 1995, ch. 719, sec. 7)

Sec. 406.011. Reappointment. (a) Not earlier than 90 days prior to the expiration date of the notary's term, a notary public may apply for reappointment on submission of a new application to the secretary of state.

(b) A notary public who is not reappointed on or before the expiration date of the term the notary public is serving will be appointed for a new term expiring four years from the date of qualification. (1987, ch. 147, sec. 1; 1995, ch. 719, sec. 8)

Sec. 406.012. Inspection of Records. All records concerning the appointment and qualification of the notary public shall be kept in the office of the secretary of state. The records are public information. (1987, ch. 147, sec. 1; 1989, ch. 4, sec. 2.16)

Sec. 406.013. Seal. (a) A notary public shall provide a seal of office that clearly shows, when embossed, stamped, or printed on a document, the words "Notary Public, State of Texas" around a star of five points, the notary public's name, and the date the notary public's commission expires. The notary public shall authenticate all official acts with the seal of office.

(b) The seal may be a circular form not more than two inches in diameter or a rectangular form not more than one inch in width and 2-1/2 inches in length. The seal must have a serrated or milled edge border.

(c) The seal must be affixed by a seal press or stamp that embosses or prints a seal that legibly reproduced the required elements of the seal under photographic methods. An indelible ink pad must be used for affixing by a stamp the impression of a seal on an instrument to authenticate the notary public's official act.

(d) Repealed by Acts 1989, 71st Leg., Ch. 4, Sec. 2.71(d), eff. Sept. 1, 1989. (1987, ch. 147, sec. 1; 1989, ch. 4, sec. 2.71(d))

Sec. 406.014. Notary Records. (a) A notary public other than a court clerk notarizing instruments for the court shall keep in a book a record of:

(1) the date of each instrument notarized;

(2) the date of the notarization;

(3) the name of the signer, grantor, or maker;

(4) the signer's, grantor's, or maker's residence or alleged residence;

(5) whether the signer, grantor, or maker is personally known by the notary public, was identified by an identification card issued by a governmental agency or a passport issued by the United States, or was introduced to the notary public and, if introduced, the name and residence or alleged residence of the individual introducing the signer, grantor, or maker.

(6) if the instrument is proved by a witness, the residence of the witness, whether the witness is personally known by the notary public or was introduced to the notary public and, if introduced, the name and residence of the individual introducing the witness;

(7) the name and residence of the grantee;

(8) if land is conveyed or charged by the instrument, the name of the original grantee and the county where the land is located; and

(9) a brief description of the instrument.

(b) Entries in the notary's book are public information.

(c) A notary public shall, on payment of all fees, provide a certified copy of any record in the notary public's office to any person requesting the copy.

(d) A notary public who administers an oath pursuant to Article 45.01, Code of Criminal Procedure, is exempt from the requirement in Subsection (a) of recording that oath. (1987, ch. 147, sec. 1; 1989, ch. 4, sec. 2.17(a); 1989, ch. 406, sec. 2; 1989, ch. 451, sec. 1)

Sec. 406.015. Copies Certified by County Clerk. (a) A copy of a record, declaration, protest, or other official act of the notary public may be certified by the county clerk with whom the instrument is deposited.

(b) A copy of an instrument certified by the county clerk under Subsection (a) has the same authority as if certified by the notary public by whom the record, declaration, protest, or other official act was originally made. (1987, ch. 147, sec. 1))

Sec. 406.016. Authority. (a) A notary public has the same authority as the county clerk to:

(1) take acknowledgments or proofs of written instruments;

(2) protest instruments permitted by law to be protested;

(3) administer oaths;

(4) take depositions; and

(5) certify copies of documents not recordable in the public records.

(b) A notary public shall sign an instrument in Subsection (a) in the name under which the notary public is commissioned.

(c) A notary public may not issue an identification card.

(d) A notary public not licensed to practice law in this state may not give legal advice or accept fees for legal advice. (1987, ch. 147, sec. 1)

Sec. 406.0165. Signing Document for Individual with Disability. (a) A notary may sign the name of an individual who is physically unable to sign or make a mark on a document presented for notarization if directed to do so by that individual, in the presence of a witness who has no legal or equitable interest in any real or personal property that is the subject of, or is affected by, the document being signed. The notary shall require identification of the witness in the same manner as from an acknowledging person under Section 121.005, Civil Practices and Remedies Code.

(b) A notary who signs a document under this section shall write, beneath the signature, the following or a substantially similar sentence:

"Signature affixed by notary in the presence of (name of witness), a disinterested witness, under Section 406.0165, Government Code."

(c) A signature made under this section is effective as the signature of the individual on whose behalf the signature was made for any purpose. A subsequent bona fide purchaser for value may rely on the signature of the notary as evidence of the individual's consent to execution of the document.

(d) In this section, "disability" means a physical impairment that impedes the ability to sign or make a mark on a document. (1997, ch. 1218, sec. 1)

Sec. 406.017. Representation as Attorney. (a) A notary public who is not an attorney and who advertises the services of a notary public in a language other than English, whether by signs, pamphlets, stationery, or other written communication or by radio or television, shall post or otherwise include with the advertisement a notice that the notary public is not an attorney.

(b) The notice must be in English and in the language of the advertisement and in letters of a conspicuous size. If the advertisement is by radio or television, the statement may be modified, but must include substantially the same message. The notice must include the fees that a notary public may charge and the following statement:

"I AM NOT AN ATTORNEY LICENSED TO PRACTICE LAW IN TEXAS AND MAY NOT GIVE LEGAL ADVICE OR ACCEPT FEES FOR LEGAL ADVICE."

(c) Literal translation of the phrase "Notary Public" into Spanish is prohibited. In this subsection, "literal translation" means the translation of a word or phrase without regard to the true meaning of the word or phrase in the language that is being translated.

(d) Failure to comply with this section is, in addition to a violation of any other applicable law of this state, a deceptive trade practice actionable under Chapter 17, Business & Commerce Code. (1987, ch. 147, sec. 1)

Sec. 406.018. Removal from Office. (a) A notary public guilty of wilful neglect of duty or malfeasance in office may be removed from office in the manner provided by law.

(b) A notary public indicted for and convicted of a wilful neglect of duty or official misconduct shall be removed from office. The court shall include the order for removal as part of its judgment. (1987, ch. 147, sec. 1)

Sec. 406.019. Change of Address. A notary public shall notify the secretary of state of a change of the notary public's address not later than the 10th day after the date on which the change is made. (1987, ch. 147, sec. 1)

Sec. 406.020. Removal from State. A notary public who removes his residence from this state vacates the office. (1987, ch. 147, sec. 1)

Sec. 406.021. Removal from Precinct. An ex officio notary public who moves permanently from the notary public's precinct vacates the office. (1987, ch. 147, sec. 1)

Sec. 406.022. Effect of Vacancy. If the office of a notary public becomes vacant due to resignation, removal, or death, the county clerk of the county in which the notary public resides shall obtain the record books and public papers belonging to the office of the notary public and deposit them in the county clerk's office. (1987, ch. 147, sec. 1; 1989, ch. 406, sec. 3)

Sec. 406.023. Administration and Enforcement. (a) The secretary of state shall adopt rules necessary for the administration and enforcement of this subchapter. The rules must be consistent with the provisions of this subchapter.

(b) The secretary of state may employ an investigator to aid in the enforcement of this subchapter.

(c) The secretary of state may provide for the appointment of county clerks as deputy custodians for the limited authentication of notary public records deposited in the clerks' offices. (1987, ch. 147, sec. 1)

Sec. 406.024. Fees Charged by Notary Public. (a) A notary public may charge the following fees:

(1) for protesting a bill or note for nonacceptance or nonpayment, register and seal, a fee of $4;

(2) for each notice of protest, a fee of $1;

(3) for protesting in all other cases, a fee of $4;

(4) for certificate and seal to a protest, a fee of $4;

(5) for taking the acknowledgment or proof of a deed or other instrument in writing, for registration, including certificate and seal, a fee of $6 for the first signature and $1 for each additional signature;

(6) for administering an oath or affirmation with certificate and seal, a fee of $6;

(7) for a certificate under seal not otherwise provided for, a fee of $6;

(8) for a copy of a record or paper in the notary public's office, a fee of 50 cents for each page;

(9) for taking the deposition of a witness, 50 cents for each 100 words;

(10) for swearing a witness to a deposition, certificate, seal, and other business connected with taking the deposition, a fee of $6; and

(11) for a notarial act not provided for, a fee of $6.

(b) A notary public may charge a fee only for an acknowledgment or official act under Subsection (a). The fee charged may not exceed the fee authorized by Subsection (a). (1987, ch. 147, sec. 1; 1989, ch. 4, sec. 2.18(a); 1995, ch. 259, sec. 1)

Sec. 406.025. Signature on Commission After Change in Office. If the governor or secretary of state ceases to hold or perform the duties of office, existing stocks of commissions bearing the person's printed name, signature, or facsimile signature may be used until they are exhausted, and the person succeeding to the office or the duties of the office shall have the commissions issued with:

(1) the obsolete printed name, signature, or facsimile signature struck through;

(2) the successor's printed name submitted for the obsolete printed name, signature, or facsimile signature; and

(3) the inscription "Printed name authorized by law" near the successor's printed name. (1995, ch. 719, sec. 9)

Subchapter B. Commissioner of Deeds

Sec. 406.051. Appointment. (a) The governor may biennially appoint and commission one or more individuals in other states, territories, or foreign countries or in the District of Columbia to serve as commissioner of deeds.

(b) An appointment may be made only on the recommendation of the executive authority of the state, territory, or foreign country or the District of Columbia. (1987, ch. 147, sec. 1)

Sec. 406.052. Term. The term of office of a commissioner of deeds is two years. (1987, ch. 147, sec. 1)

Sec. 406.053. Oath. Before performing the duties of office, a commissioner of deeds shall take and subscribe an oath to well and faithfully perform the duties of office under the laws of this state. The oath shall be:

(1) taken before the clerk of a court of record in the city, county, or country in which the commissioner resides;

(2) certified to by the clerk under the clerk's hand and seal of office; and

(3) filed in the office of the secretary of state of this state. (1987, ch. 147, sec. 1)

Sec. 406.054. Seal. A commissioner of deeds shall provide a seal with a star of five points in the center and the words "Commissioner of the State of Texas" engraved on the seal. The seal shall be used to certify all official acts of the commissioner of deeds. An instrument that does not have the impression of the seal, or an act of the commissioner of deeds that is not certified by the impression of the seal, is not valid in this state. (1987, ch. 147, sec. 1)

Sec. 406.055. Authority. A commissioner of deeds has the same authority as a notary public to take acknowledgments and proofs of written instruments, to administer oaths, and to take depositions to be used or recorded in this state. (1987, ch. 147, sec. 1)

Title 6. Public Officers and Employees
Subtitle A. Provisions Generally Applicable to Public Officer and Employees
Chapter 603. Provisions of Documents and Fees of Office

Sec. 603.001. Definition
Sec. 603.006. Fee Book
Sec. 603.007. Bill for Fees
Sec. 603.008. Posting of Fees Required
Sec. 603.010. Overcharging of Fees; Penalty

Sec. 603.001. Definition. In this chapter, "document" includes any instrument, paper, or other record. (1993, ch. 268, sec. 1)

Sec. 603.006. Fee Book. An officer who by law may charge a fee for a service shall keep a fee book and shall enter in the book all fees charged for services rendered. (1993, ch. 268, sec. 1; Formerly T.R.C.S., Article 3907)

Sec. 603.007. Bill for Fees. A fee under this chapter is not payable to a person until a clerk or officer produces, or is ready to produce, a bill in writing containing the details of the fee to the person who owes the fee. The bill must be signed by the clerk or officer to whom the fee is due or who charges the fee or by the successor in office or legal representative of the clerk or officer. (1993, ch. 268, sec. 1; Formerly T.R.C.S., Article 3908)

Sec. 603.008. Posting of Fees Required. A county judge, clerk of a district or county court, sheriff, justice of the peace, constable, or notary public shall keep posted at all times in a conspicuous place in the respective offices a complete list of fees the person may charge by law. (1993, ch. 268, sec. 1; Formerly T.R.C.S., Article 3910)

Sec. 603.010. Overcharging of Fees; Penalty. An officer named in this chapter who demands and receives a higher fee than authorized under this chapter or a fee that is not authorized under this chapter is liable to the aggrieved person for four times the amount unlawfully demanded and received. (1993, ch. 268, sec. 1; Formerly T.R.C.S., Article 3909)

Texas Civil Practice and Remedies Code
Title 6. Miscellaneous Provisions
Chapter 121. Acknowledgments and Proofs of Written Instruments

Sec. 121.001. Officers Who May Take Acknowledgments and Proofs
Sec. 121.002. Corporate Acknowledgments
Sec. 121.003. Authority of Officers
Sec. 121.004. Method of Acknowledgment
Sec. 121.005. Proof of Identity of Acknowledging Person
Sec. 121.006. Alteration of Authorized Forms; Definition.
Sec. 121.007. Form for Ordinary Certificate of Acknowledgment
Sec. 121.008. Short Forms for Certificates of Acknowledgment
Sec. 121.009. Proof of Acknowledgment by Witness
Sec. 121.010. Form of Certificate for Proof by Witness
Sec. 121.011. Proof of Acknowledgment by Handwriting
Sec. 121.012. Record of Acknowledgment
Sec. 121.013. Subpoena of Witness; Attachment
Sec. 121.014. Action for Damages

Sec. 121.001. Officers Who May Take Acknowledgments and Proofs. (a) An acknowledgment or proof of a written instrument may be taken in this state by:
 (1) a clerk of a district court;
 (2) a judge or clerk of a county court; or
 (3) a notary public; or
 (4) a county tax assessor-collector or an employee of the county tax assessor-collector if the instrument is required or authorized to be filed in the office of the county tax assessor-collector.
 (b) An acknowledgment or proof of a written instrument may be taken outside this state, but inside the United States or its territories, by:
 (1) a clerk of a court of record having a seal;
 (2) a commissioner of deeds appointed under the laws of this state; or
 (3) a notary public.

(c) An acknowledgment or proof of a written instrument may be taken outside the United States and its territories by:

(1) A minister, commissioner, or charge d'affaires of the United States who is a resident of and is accredited in the country where the acknowledgment or proof is taken;

(2) a consul-general, consul, vice-consul, commercial agent, vice-commercial agent, deputy consul, or consular agent of the United States who is a resident of the country where the acknowledgment or proof is taken; or

(3) a notary public or any other official authorized to administer oaths in the jurisdiction where the acknowledgment or proof is taken.

(d) A commissioned officer of the United States Armed Forces or of a United States Armed Forces Auxiliary may take acknowledgment or proof of a written instrument of a member of the armed forces, a member of an armed forces auxiliary, or a member's spouse. If an acknowledgment or proof is taken under this subsection, it is presumed, absent pleading and proof to the contrary, that the commissioned officer who signed was a commissioned officer on the date that the officer signed, and that the acknowledging person was a member of the authorized group of military personnel or spouses. The failure of the commissioned officer to attach an official seal to the certificate of acknowledgment or proof of an instrument does not invalidate the acknowledgment or proof. (1985, ch. 959, sec. 1; 1987, ch. 891, sec. 1; 1995, ch. 165, sec. 18)

Sec. 121.002. Corporate Acknowledgments. (a) An employee of a corporation is not disqualified because of his employment from taking an acknowledgment or proof of a written instrument in which the corporation has an interest.

(b) An officer who is a shareholder in a corporation is not disqualified from taking an acknowledgment or proof of an instrument in which the corporation has an interest unless: (1) the corporation has 1,000 or fewer shareholders; and (2) the officer owns more than one-tenth of one percent of the issued and outstanding stock. (1985, ch. 959, sec. 1)

Sec 121.003. Authority of Officers. In a proceeding to prove a written instrument, an officer authorized by this chapter to take an acknowledgment or proof of a written instrument is also authorized to:

(1) administer oaths;

(2) employ and swear interpreters; and

(3) issue subpoenas. (1985, ch. 959, sec. 1)

Sec. 121.004. Method of Acknowledgment. (a) To acknowledge a written instrument for recording, the grantor or person who executed the instrument must appear before an officer and must state that he executed the instrument for the purposes and consideration expressed in it.

(b) The officer shall:

(1) make a certificate of acknowledgment;

(2) sign the certificate; and

(3) seal the certificate with the seal of office.

(c) The failure of a notary public to attach an official seal to a certificate of an acknowledgment or proof of a written instrument made outside this state but inside the United States or its territories renders the acknowledgment or proof invalid only if the jurisdiction in which the certificate is made required the notary public to attach the seal. (1985, ch. 959, sec. 1; 1995, ch. 603, sec. 1)

Sec. 121.005. Proof of Identity of Acknowledging Person. (a) An officer may not take the acknowledgment of a written instrument unless the officer knows or has satisfactory evidence that the acknowledging person is the person who executed the instrument and is described in it. An officer may accept, as satisfactory evidence of the identity of an acknowledging person, only:

(1) the oath of a credible witness personally known to the officer; or

(2) a current identification card or other document issued by the federal government or any state government that contains the photograph and signature of the acknowledging person.

(b) Except in a short form certificate of acknowledgment authorized by Section 121.008, the officer must note in the certificate of acknowledgment that:

(1) he personally knows the acknowledging person; or

(2) evidence of a witness or an identification card or other document was used to identify the acknowledging person. (1985, ch. 959, sec. 1; 1997, ch. 90, sec. 1)

Sec. 121.006. Alteration of Authorized Forms; Definition. (a) An acknowledgment form provided by this chapter may be altered as circumstances require. The authorization of a form does not prevent the use of other forms. The marital status or other status of the acknowledging person may be shown after the person's name..

(b) In acknowledgment form "acknowledged" means:

(1) in the case of a natural person, that the person personally appeared before the officer taking the acknowledgment and acknowledged executing the instrument for the purposes and consideration expressed in it;

(2) in the case of a person as principal by an attorney-in-fact for the principal, that the attorney-in-fact personally appeared before the officer taking the acknowledgment and that the attorney-in-fact acknowledged executing the instrument as the act of the principal for the purposes and consideration expressed in it;

(3) in the case of a partnership by a partner or partners acting for the partnership, that the partner or partners personally appeared before the officer taking the acknowledgment and acknowledged executing the instrument as the act of the partnership for the purposes and consideration expressed in it;

(4) in the case of a corporation by a corporate officer or agent, that the corporate officer or agent personally appeared before the officer taking the acknowledgment and that the corporate officer of agent acknowledged executing the instrument in the capacity stated, as the act of the corporation, for the purposes and consideration expressed in it; and

(5) in the case of a person acknowledging as a public officer, trustee, executor or administrator of an estate, guardian, or other representative, that the person personally appeared before the officer taking the acknowledgment and acknowledged executing the instrument by proper authority in the capacity stated and for the purposes and consideration expressed in it. (1985, ch. 959, sec. 1)

Sec. 121.007. Form for Ordinary Certificate of Acknowledgment. The form of an ordinary certificate of acknowledgment must be substantially as follows:

"The State of _____,
"County of _____,

"Before me _____ (here insert the name and character of the officer) on this day personally appeared _____, known to me (or proved to me on the oath of _____ or through _____ (description of identity card or other document)) to be the person whose name is subscribed to the foregoing instrument and acknowledged to me that he executed the same for the purposes and consideration therein expressed.

(Seal) "Given under my hand and seal of office this _____ day of _____, A.D., _____."

(1985, ch. 959, sec. 1; 1997, ch. 90, sec. 1)

Sec. 121.008. Short Forms for Certificate of Acknowledgment. (a) The forms for certificates of acknowledgment provided by this section may be used as alternatives to other authorized forms. They may be referred to as "statutory forms of acknowledgment."

(b) Short forms for certificates of acknowledgment include:

(1) For a natural person acting in his own right.

State of _____
County of _____
This instrument was acknowledged before me on _____ (date) by _____ (name or names of person or persons acknowledging).
(Signature of officer)
(Title of officer)
My commission expires: _____

(2) For a natural person as principal acting by attorney-in-fact:

State of _____
County of _____
This instrument was acknowledged before me on _____ (date) by _____ (name of attorney-in-fact) as attorney-in-fact on behalf of _____ (name of principal).
(Signature of officer)
(Title of officer)
My commission expires: _____

(3) For a partnership acting by one or more partners:

State of _____
County of _____
This instrument was acknowledged before me on _____ (date) by _____ (name of acknowledging partner or partners), partner(s) on behalf of _____ (name of partnership), a partnership.
(Signature of officer)
(Title of officer)
My commission expires: _____

(4) For a corporation:

TEXAS NOTARY LAW PRIMER

State of _____
County of _____
This instrument was acknowledged before me on _____
(date) by _____ (name of officer), (title of officer) of (name of corporation acknowledging) a _____ (state of incorporation) corporation, on behalf of said corporation.
(Signature of officer)
(Title of officer)
My commission expires: _____

(5) For a public officer, trustee, executor, administrator, guardian, or other representative:

State of _____
County of _____
This instrument was acknowledged before me on _____
(date) by_____ (name of representative) as _____ (title of representative) of _____ (name of entity or person represented).
(Signature of officer)
(Title of officer)
My commission expires: _____
(1985, ch. 959, sec. 1)

Sec. 121.009. Proof of Acknowledgment by Witness. (a) To prove a written instrument for recording, at least one of the witnesses who signed the instrument must personally appear before an officer who is authorized by this chapter to take acknowledgments or proofs and must swear:

(1) either that he saw the grantor or person who executed the instrument sign it or that that person acknowledged in the presence of the witness that he executed the instrument for the purposes and consideration expressed in it; and

(2) that he signed the instrument at the request of the grantor or person who executed the instrument.

(b) The officer must make a certificate of the testimony of the witness and must sign and officially seal the certificate.

(c) The officer may take the testimony of a witness only if the officer personally knows or has satisfactory evidence on the oath of a credible witness that the individual testifying is the person who signed the instrument as a witness that the individual testifying is the person who signed the instrument as a witness. If evidence is used to identify the witness who signed the instrument, the officer must note the use of the evidence in the certificate of acknowledgment. (1985, ch. 959, sec. 1)

Sec. 121.010. Form of Certificate for Proof by Witness. When the execution of a written instrument is proved by a witness, the certificate of the officer must be substantially as follows:

"The State of _____,
"County of _____,
"Before me, _____ (here insert the name and character of the officer), on this day personally appeared _____, known to me

(or proved to me on the oath of _____), to be the person whose name is subscribed as a witness to the foregoing instrument of writing, and after being duly sworn by me stated on oath that he saw_____, the grantor or person who executed the foregoing instrument, subscribe the same (or that the grantor or person who executed such instrument of writing acknowledged in his presence that he had executed the same for the purposes and consideration therein expressed), and that he had signed the same as a witness at the request of the grantor (or person who executed the same).
(Seal) "Given under my hand and seal of office this _____ day of _____, A.D., _____."
(1985, ch. 959, sec. 1)

Sec. 121.011. Proof of Acknowledgment by Handwriting. (a) The execution of an instrument may be established for recording by proof of the handwriting of persons who signed the instrument only if:

(1) the grantor of the instrument and all of the witnesses are dead;

(2) the grantor and all of the witnesses are not residents of this state;

(3) the residences of the grantor and the witnesses are unknown to the person seeking to prove the instrument and cannot be ascertained;

(4) the witnesses have become legally incompetent to testify; or

(5) the grantor of the instrument refuses to acknowledge the execution of the instrument and all of the witnesses are dead, not residents of this state, or legally incompetent or their places of residence are unknown.

(b) If the grantor or person who executed the instrument signed his name to the instrument, its execution must be proved by evidence of the handwriting of that person and at least one witness who signed the instrument. If the grantor or person who executed the instrument signed the instrument by making his mark, its execution must be proved by the handwriting of at least two of the witnesses who signed the instrument.

(c) Evidence taken for proof of handwriting must give the residence of the testifying witness. A testifying witness must have known the person whose handwriting is being proved and must be well acquainted with the handwriting in question and recognize it as genuine.

(d) Evidence offered for proof of handwriting must be given in writing by the deposition or affidavit of two or more disinterested persons. The evidence must satisfactorily prove to the officer each of the requirements provided by this section. The officer taking the proof must certify the witnesses' testimony. The officer must sign, officially seal, and attach this certificate to the instrument with the depositions or affidavits of the witnesses. (1985, ch. 959, sec. 1)

Sec. 121.012. Record of Acknowledgment. (a) An officer authorized by law to take an acknowledgment or proof of a written instrument required or permitted by law to be recorded must enter in a well-bound book and officially sign a short statement of each acknowledgment or proof. The statement must contain the date that the acknowledgment or proof was taken, the date of the instrument, and the names of the grantor and grantee of the instrument.

(b) If the execution of the instrument is acknowledged by the grantor of the instrument, the statement must also contain:

(1) the grantor's known or alleged residence;

(2) whether the grantor is personally known to the officer; and

(3) if the grantor is unknown to the officer, the name and residence of the person who introduced the grantor to the officer, if any.

(c) If the execution of the instrument is proved by a witness who signed the instrument, the statement must also contain:

(1) the name of the witness;

(2) the known or alleged residence of the witness;

(3) whether the witness is personally known to the officer; and

(4) if the witness is unknown to the officer, the name and known or alleged residence of the person who introduced the witness to the officer, if any.

(d) If land is charged or conveyed by the instrument, the statement must also contain:

(1) the name of the original grantee; and

(2) the name of the county in which the land is located.

(e) The statements of acknowledgment recorded by the officer are original public records, open for public inspection and examination at all reasonable times. The officer must deliver the book to his successor in office. (1985, ch. 959, sec. 1)

Sec. 121.013. Subpoena of Witness; Attachment. (a) On the sworn application of a person interested in the proof of an instrument required or permitted by law to be recorded, stating that a witness to the instrument refuses to appear and testify regarding the execution of an instrument and that the instrument cannot be proven without the evidence of the witness, an officer authorized to take proofs of instruments shall issue a subpoena requiring the witness to appear before the officer and testify about the execution of the instrument.

(b) If the witness fails to obey the subpoena, the officer has the same powers to enforce the attendance and compel the answers of the witness as does a district judge. Attachment may not be issued, however, unless the witness receives or is tendered the same compensation that is made to witnesses in other cases. An officer may not require the witness to leave his county of residence, but if the witness is temporarily present in the county where the execution of the instrument is sought to be proven for registration, he may be required to appear. (1985, ch. 959, sec. 1)

Sec. 121.014. Action for Damages. A person injured by the failure, refusal, or neglect of an officer to comply with a provision of this chapter has a cause of action against the officer to recover damages resulting from the failure, refusal, or neglect of the officer. (1985, ch. 959, sec. 1) ■

Office of the Texas Secretary of State

Secretary of State
Notary Public Unit

Street Address: (used also for courier mail)
Secretary of State
Notary Public Unit
1019 Brazos, #214
Austin, TX 78701

Mailing Address:
Secretary of State
Notary Public Unit
P.O. Box 12079
Austin, TX 78711-2079

Telephone: 1-512-463-5705

In addition, there are many useful resources available at the state's official web site, including links to legislation, the Secretary of State's office and research bureaus. You can access the state's home page at www.state.tx.us.

You can also access the Secretary of State's office directly at www.sos.state.tx.us. Information for Notaries appears under the "Functions of Office" heading.

County Clerks' Offices

Many notarized documents — particularly deeds and mortgage documents — are publicly recorded at the local office of the County Clerk/Recorder. The addresses of these offices are listed below.

This list can be of additional use to those needing access to, or authenticated copies of, Notary records left in the custody of county clerks who have been appointed deputy custodians of notarial records (see TGC, Section 406.023).

Anderson County
500 N. Church St.
Palestine 75801
1-903-723-7406

Andrews County
201 N. Main, #104
Andrews 79714
1-915-524-1401

Angelina County
P.O. Box 908
Lufkin 75902-0908
1-409-634-5413

Aransas County
301 N. Live Oak St.
Rockport 78382
1-512-790-0100

Archer County
P.O. Box 458
Archer City 76351-0258
1-940-574-4811

Armstrong County
P.O. Box 189
Claude 79019
1-806-226-3221

Atascosa County
Courthouse, #41
Jourdanton 78026
1-830-769-3093

Austin County
1 E. Main
Bellville 77418
1-409-865-5911

Bailey County
300 S. 1st Street
Muleshoe 79347
1-806-272-3077

Bandera County
P.O. Box 877
Bandera 78003
1-830-796-3781

Bastrop County
804 Pecan St.
Bastrop 78602
1-512-303-2579

Baylor County
101 S. Washington
Seymour 76380
1-940-888-2662

Bee County
105 W. Corpus Christi St.
Beeville 78102
1-512-362-3260

Bell County
P.O. Box 768
Belton 76513
1-254-933-5105

Bexar County
100 Dolorosa St., #101
San Antonio 78205-3036
1-210-335-2626

Blanco County
P.O. Box 471
Johnson City 78636
1-830-868-4266

Borden County
P.O. Box 156
Gail 79738
1-806-756-4391

Bosque County
P.O. Box 647
Meridian 76665
1-254-435-2382

COUNTY CLERKS' OFFICES

Bowie County
710 James Bowie Dr.
New Boston 75570
1-903-628-2571

Brazoria County
111 E. Locust St., #308
Angleton 77515
1-409-849-5711

Brazos County
300 E. 26th St.
Bryan 77803
1-409-361-4102

Brewster County
P.O. Box 1630
Alpine 79831
1-915-837-2412

Briscoe County
415 Main St.
Silverton 79257
1-806-823-2131

Brooks County
P.O. Box 515
Falfurrias 78355
1-512-325-5604

Brown County
200 S. Broadway
Brownwood 76801
1-915-643-2828

Burleson County
P.O. Box 766
Caldwell 77836
1-409-567-4226

Burnet County
220 S. Pierce St.
Burnet 78611
1-512-756-5420

Caldwell County
Courthouse, #301
Lockhart 78644
1-512-398-1808

Calhoun County
211 S. Ann St.
Port Lavaca 77979
1-512-553-4600

Callahan County
100 W. 4th St., #200
Baird 79504-5323
1-915-854-1155

Cameron County
964 E. Harrison St.
Brownsville 78520
1-956-544-0830

Camp County
126 Church St., #303
Pittsburg 75686
1-903-856-3845

Carson County
500 Main St., 1st Fl.
Panhandle 79068
1-806-537-3622

Cass County
P.O. Box 825
Linden 75563
1-903-756-5181

Castro County
100 E. Bedford
Dimmitt 79027
1-806-647-4451

Chambers County
P.O. Box 939
Anahuac 77580
1-281-576-2243

Cherokee County
502 N. Main
Rusk 75785
1-903-683-2324

Childress County
100 Avenue E, NW
Childress 79201
1-940-937-2221

Clay County
100 N. Bridge
Henrietta 76365
1-940-538-4651

Cochran County
Courthouse, #105
Morton 79346
1-806-266-5508

Coke County
P.O. Box 52
Robert Lee 76945
1-915-453-2641

Coleman County
Courthouse
Coleman 76834-0512
1-915-625-4218

Collin County
210 S. McDonald St., #626
McKinney 75069
1-972-548-4635

Collingsworth County
Courthouse, 2nd Fl.
Wellington 79095
1-806-447-5408

Colorado County
400 Springs St.
Columbus 78934
1-409-732-2604

Comal County
150 N. Seguin Ave., #301
New Braunfels 78130
1-830-620-5501

Comanche County
Courthouse
Comanche 76442
1-915-356-2466

Concho County
P.O. Box 158
Paint Rock 76866
1-915-732-4321

Cooke County
100 S. Dixon
Gainesville 76240
1-940-668-5435

Coryell County
620 E. Main St.
Gatesville 76528
1-254-865-5911

Cottle County
Box 729
Paducah 79248
1-806-492-3613

Crane County
P.O. Box 457
Crane 79731
1-915-558-3589

Crockett County
P.O. Box 1857
Ozona 76943
1-915-392-2965

Crosby County
P.O. Box 385
Crosbyton 79322
1-806-675-2011

Culbertson County
P.O. Box 747
Van Horn 79855
1-915-283-2059

Dallam County
P.O. Box 9395
Dalhart 79022
1-806-249-2450

Dallas County
411 Elm St.
Dallas 75202
1-214-653-7555

Dawson County
2106 S. 5th St.
Lamesa 79331
1-806-872-7544

Deaf Smith County
235 E. 3rd St., #201
Hereford 79045-5593
1-806-363-7000

Delta County
200 W. Dallas Ave.
Cooper 75432
1-903-395-2211

Denton County
110 W. Hickory St., #207
Denton 76201
1-940-565-8687

De Witt County
307 N. Gonzales St.
Cuero 77954
1-512-275-2116

Dickens County
P.O. Box 179
Dickens 79229
1-806-623-5532

Dimmit County
103 N. 5th St.
Carrizo Springs 78834
1-830-876-2323

Donley County
P.O. Box 909
Clarendon 79226
1-806-874-3625

Duval County
P.O. Box 189
San Diego 78384
1-512-279-3322

Eastland County
P.O. Box 327
Eastland 76448
1-254-629-1263

Ector County
300 N. Grant St., #227
Odessa 79761
1-915-335-3030

Edwards County
P. O. Box 348
Rocksprings 78880
1-830-683-6122

Ellis County
101 W. Main St.
Waxahachie 75165
1-972-923-5011

El Paso County
500 E. San Antonio St.
El Paso 79901
1-915-546-2098

Erath County
100 Graham St.
Stephenville 76401
1-254-965-1452

Falls County
P.O. Box 458
Marlin 76661
1-817-883-3182

Fannin County
101 E. Sam Rayburn Dr.
Bonham 75418
1-903-583-7455

Fayette County
151 N. Washington
La Grange 78945
1-409-968-6469

Fisher County
P.O. Box 306
Roby 79543
1-915-776-2151

Floyd County
Courthouse, #105
Floydada 79235
1-806-983-4905

Foard County
P.O. Box 660
Crowell 79227
1-940-684-1424

Fort Bend County
301 Jackson, #719
Richmond 77469
1-281-341-8608

Franklin County
P.O. Box 577
Mount Vernon 75457
1-903-537-2342

Freestone County
Courthouse, #307
Fairfield 75840
1-903-389-3335

Frio County
500 E. San Antonio, #7
Pearsall 78061-3100
1-830-334-2154

Gaines County
P.O. Box 847
Seminole 79360
1-915-758-5411

Galveston County
722 Moody
Galveston 77550
1-409-766-2244

Garza County
300 W. Main
Post 79356
1-806-495-4405

Gillespie County
101 W. Main St., #9
Fredericksburg 78624
1-830-997-7502

Glasscock County
P.O. Box 67
Garden City 79739
1-915-354-2382

Goliad County
P.O. Box 677
Goliad 77963
1-512-645-3337

Gonzales County
P.O. Box 80
Gonzales 78629
1-830-672-2327

Gray County
205 N. Russell St.
Pampa 79065
1-806-669-8007

COUNTY CLERKS' OFFICES

Grayson County
100 W. Houston St., #15
Sherman 75090
1-903-813-4228

Gregg County
101 E. Methvin St., #300
Longview 75601-7214
1-903-236-8420

Grimes County
P.O. Box 160
Anderson 77830
1-409-873-2111

Guadalupe County
307 W. Court St.
Seguin 78155
1-830-303-4188

Hale County
500 Broadway, #100
Plainview 79072-8050
1-806-291-5214

Hall County
Courthouse
Memphis 79245
1-806-259-2511

Hamilton County
Courthouse
Hamilton 76531
1-254-386-3815

Hansford County
P.O. Box 367
Spearman 79081
1-806-659-4100

Hardeman County
P.O. Box 30
Quanah 79252
1-940-633-2911

Hardin County
P.O. Box 760
Kountze 77625
1-409-246-5120

Harris County
1001 Preston Rd., #911
Houston 77002
1-713-755-4000

Harrison County
Courthouse, 3rd Fl.
Marshall 75670
1-903-935-4805

Hartley County
Drawer G
Channing 79018
1-806-235-3442

Haskell County
P.O. Box 905
Haskell 79521
1-940-864-2851

Hays County
102 N. LBJ Dr., #300
San Marcos 78666
1-512-392-2521

Hemphill County
400 Main St.
Canadian 79014
1-806-323-6521

Henderson County
101 E. Tyler St.
Athens 75751
1-903-675-6120

Hidalgo County
P.O. Box 1356
Eninburg 78540-1356
1-956-318-2600

Hill County
P.O. Box 457
Hillsboro 76645
1-254-582-2371

Hockley County
802 Houston St., #101
Levelland 79336
1-806-894-6856

Hood County
Courthouse, #7
Granbury 76048
1-817-579-3200

Hopkins County
P.O. Box 288
Sulphur Springs
75483-0288
1-903-885-3926

Houston County
P.O. Box 370
Crockett 75835
1-409-544-3255

Howard County
300 Main, #207
Big Spring 79720
1-915-264-2202

Hudspeth County
P.O. Box 68
Sierra Blanca 79851
1-915-369-2321

Hunt County
P.O. Box 1097
Greenville 75403-1097
1-903-408-4146

Hutchinson County
P.O. Box 790
Stinnett 79083
1-806-878-4000

Irion County
P.O. Box 770
Mertzon 76941
1-915-835-4361

Jack County
100 Main St.
Jacksboro 76458
1-940-567-2241

Jackson County
115 W. Main St.
Edna 77957
1-512-782-2352

Jasper County
Courthouse, #101
Jasper 75951
1-409-384-2612

Jeff Davis County
P.O. Box 836
Fort Davis 79734
1-915-426-3968

Jefferson County
P.O. Box 4025
Beaumont 77704
1-409-835-8466

Jim Hogg County
P.O. Box 729
Hebbronville 78361
1-512-527-3015

Jim Wells County
200 N. Almond St.
Alice 78332
1-512-668-5706

Johnson County
2 Main St.
Cleburne 79031
1-940-556-6360

TEXAS NOTARY LAW PRIMER

Jones County
P.O. Box 148
Anson 79501
1-915-823-3741

Karnes County
101 N. Panna Maria Ave.
Karnes City 78118-2988
1-830-780-3732

Kaufman County
100 W. Mulberry
Kaufman 75142
1-972-932-4331

Kendall County
204 E. San Antonio, #1
Boerne 78006
1-830-249-9343

Kenedy County
P.O. Box 989
Raymondville 78580
1-956-689-5674

Kent County
P.O. Box 6
Jayton 79528
1-806-237-3373

Kerr County
700 Main St.
Kerrville 78028
1-830-792-2211

Kimble County
501 Main St.
Junction 76849
1-915-466-2724

King County
Hwy. 82, P.O. Box 127
Guthrie 79236
1-806-596-4411

Kinney County
P.O. Box 348
Brackettville 78832
1-830-563-2401

Kleberg County
700 E. Kleberg
Kingsville 78364
1-512-595-8585

Knox County
P.O. Box 77
Benjamin 79505
1-940-454-2191

Lamar County
119 N. Main, #201
Paris 75460
1-903-737-2410

Lamb County
100 6th St., #101
Littlefield 79339
1-806-385-4222

Lampasas County
P.O. Box 231
Lampasas 76550
1-512-556-8271

La Salle County
101 Courthouse Sq.
Cotulla 78014
1-830-879-3033

Lavaca County
P.O. Box 243
Hallettsville 77964
1-512-798-2301

Lee County
P.O. Box 390
Giddings 78942
1-409-542-3178

Leon County
P.O. Box 429
Centerville 75833
1-903-536-2331

Liberty County
1923 Sam Houston, #201
Liberty 77575
1-409-336-4665

Limestone County
P.O. Box 469
Groesbeck 76642
1-254-729-3810

Lipscomb County
P.O. Box 69
Lipscomb 79056
1-806-862-4131

Live Oak County
P.O. Box 487
George West 78022
1-512-449-2733

Llano County
801 Ford St., #101
Llano 78643
1-915-247-5054

Loving County
P.O. Box 193
Mentone 79754
1-915-377-2362

Lubbock County
P.O. Box 10536
Lubbock 79408
1-806-775-1086

Lynn County
P.O. Box 1256
Tahoka 79373
1-806-998-4222

Madison County
101 W. Main St., #110
Madisonville 77864
1-409-348-2670

Marion County
102 W. Austin St., #205
Jefferson 75657
1-903-665-3261

Martin County
P.O. Box 1330
Stanton 79782
1-915-756-2231

Mason County
P.O. Box 56
Mason 76856
1-915-347-5556

Matagorda County
1700 7th St., #301
Bay City 77414
1-409-244-7605

Maverick County
P.O. Box 955
Eagle Pass 78852
1-830-773-3824

McCulloch County
Courthouse
Brady 76825
1-915-597-0733

McLennan County
Courthouse, #214
Waco 76703-1728
1-254-757-5049

McMullen County
P.O. Box 237
Tilden 78072
1-512-274-3341

COUNTY CLERKS' OFFICES

Medina County
Courthouse, #101
Hondo 78861
1-830-741-6020

Menard County
P.O. Box 1028
Menard 76859
1-915-396-4789

Midland County
200 W. Wall St.
Midland 79701
1-915-688-1148

Milam County
P.O. Box 1008
Cameron 76520
1-254-697-3581

Mills County
P.O. Box 483
Goldthwaite 76844
1-915-648-2222

Mitchell County
349 Oak St.
Colorado City 79512
1-915-728-8439

Montague County
P.O. Box 475
Montague 76251
1-940-894-2401

Montgomery County
301 N. Thompson, #210
Conroe 77301
1-409-539-7812

Moore County
715 S. Dumas Ave., #202
Dumas 79029
1-806-935-5588

Morris County
500 Broadnax St.
Daingerfield 75638
1-903-645-3691

Motley County
P.O. Box 719
Matador 79244
1-806-347-2334

Nacogdoches County
101 W. Main St.
Nacogdoches 75961
1-409-560-7755

Navarro County
300 W. 3rd Ave., #102
Corsicana 75110
1-903-654-3024

Newton County
P.O. Box J
Newton 75966
1-409-379-5691

Nolan County
P.O. Box 1201
Sweetwater 79556-1201
1-915-235-2263

Nueces County
901 Leopard St., #301
Corpus Christi 78401
1-512-888-0444

Ochiltree County
511 S. Main
Perryton 79070
1-806-435-8075

Oldham County
P.O. Box 195
Vega 79092
1-806-267-2607

Orange County
801 W. Division St.
Orange 77630
1-409-883-7740

Palo Pinto County
P.O. Box 159
Palo Pinto 76484-0190
1-940-659-1253

Panola County
Courthouse, #216-A
Carthage 75633
1-903-693-0391

Parker County
1 Courthouse Sq.
Weatherford 76086
1-817-599-6591

Parmer County
P.O. Box 506
Farwell 79325
1-806-481-3383

Pecos County
103 W. Callaghan
Fort Stockton 79735
1-915-336-2792

Polk County
Courthouse, 3rd Fl.
Livingston 77351
1-409-327-6813

Potter County
500 S. Fillmore
Amarillo 79101
1-806-379-2250

Presidio County
P.O. Box 606
Marfa 79843
1-915-729-4452

Rains County
P.O. Box 158
Emory 75440
1-903-473-2555

Randall County
401 16th St.
Canyon 79015
1-806-655-6270

Reagan County
P.O. Box 100
Big Lake 76932
1-915-884-2665

Real County
P.O. Box M
Leakey 78873
1-830-232-5304

Red River County
200 N. Walnut St.
Clarksville 75426
1-903-427-2680

Reeves County
100. E. 4th St.
Pecos 79772
1-915-445-5418

Refugio County
808 Commerce, #104
Refugio 78377
1-512-526-4434

Roberts County
P.O. Box 478
Miami 79059
1-806-868-3721

Robertson County
P.O. Box 427
Franklin 77856
1-409-828-3542

Rockwall County
1101 Ridge Rd., #206
Rockwall 75087
1-972-882-0240

Runnels County
600 Courthouse Sq.
Ballinger 76821
1-915-365-2633

Rusk County
115 N. Main St.
Henderson 75652
1-903-657-0302

Sabine County
P.O. Box 716
Hemphill 75948
1-409-787-3543

San Augustine Co.
203 Courthouse
San Augustine 75972
1-409-275-2762

San Jacinto County
P.O. Box 944
Coldspring 77331
1-409-653-4331

San Patricio County
400 W. Sinton St., #105
Sinton 78387
1-512-364-6120

San Saba County
Courthouse
San Saba 76877
1-915-372-3635

Schleicher County
P.O. Box 536
Eldorado 76936
1-915-853-2766

Scurry County
1806 25th St.
Snyder 79549
1-915-573-8576

Shackelford County
P.O. Box 1614
Albany 76430
1-915-762-2232

Shelby County
200 San Augustine, #6
Center 75935
1-409-598-3863

Sherman County
P.O. Box 165
Stratford 79084
1-806-396-2021

Smith County
100 N. Broadway St.
Tyler 75702
1-903-535-0575

Somervell County
P.O. Box 851
Glen Rose 76043
1-254-897-2322

Starr County
Courthouse
Rio Grande City 78582
1-956-487-2307

Stephens County
Courthouse
Breckenridge 76424
1-254-559-2190

Sterling County
P.O. Box 819
Sterling City 76951
1-915-378-3481

Stonewell County
P.O. Box 366
Aspermont 79502
1-940-989-3393

Sutton County
P.O. Box 1212
Sonora 76950
1-915-387-2711

Swisher County
Courthouse
Tulia 79088
1-806-995-3504

Tarrant County
100 E. Weatherford St.
Fort Worth 76196-0101
1-940-884-1441

Taylor County
300 Oak St.
Abilene 79602
1-915-674-1235

Terrell County
P.O. Box 4810
Sanderson 79848
1-915-345-2421

Terry County
500 W. Main St., #102
Brownfield 79316
1-806-637-6421

Throckmorton Co.
P.O. Box 700
Throckmorton 76483
1-940-849-3081

Titus County
100 W. 1st St., #200
Mount Pleasant 75455
1-903-577-6791

Tom Green County
112 W. Beauregard Ave.
San Angelo 76903
1-915-653-3318

Travis County
P.O. Box 1748
Austin 78767
1-512-473-9555

Trinity County
P.O. Box 457
Groveton 75845
1-409-642-1746

Tyler County
100 W. Bluff, #102
Woodville 75979
1-409-283-2141

Upshur County
P.O. Box 790
Gilmer 75644
1-903-843-4003

Upton County
P.O. Box 482
Rankin 79778
1-915-693-2321

Uvalde County
Courthouse, Box 3
Uvalde 78801
1-830-278-3216

Val Verde County
P.O. Box GG
Del Rio 78841-4250
1-830-774-7501

Van Zandt County
121 E. Dallas St., #201
Canton 75103
1-903-567-4071

COUNTY CLERKS' OFFICES

Victoria County
115 N. Bridge, #127
Victoria 77901
1-512-575-4458

Walker County
1100 University, #204
Huntsville 77340
1-409-436-4910

Waller County
836 Austin St., #203
Hempstead 77445
1-409-826-3357

Ward County
400 S. Allen St.
Monahans 79756
1-915-943-3200

Washington County
100 E. Main St., #104
Brenham 77833-3753
1-409-277-6200

Webb County
P.O. Box 29
Laredo 78042
1-956-721-2500

Wharton County
Courthouse, #100
Wharton 77488
1-409-532-4612

Wheeler County
P.O. Box 486
Wheeler 79096
1-806-826-5961

Wichita County
100 7th St., #202
Wichita Falls 76301
1-940-766-8101

Wilbarger County
1700 Wilbarger, #12
Vernon 76384
1-940-553-2300

Willacy County
Courthouse Annex
Raymondville 78580
1-512-689-3393

Williamson County
Courthouse, 2nd Fl.
Georgetown 78626
1-512-930-4457

Wilson County
1420 3rd St., #102
Floresville 78114
1-830-393-7303

Winkler County
P.O. Drawer Y
Kermit 79745
1-915-586-6658

Wise County
P.O. Box 393
Decatur 76234
1-940-627-5743

Wood County
P.O. Box 938
Quitman 75783
1-903-763-2716

Yoakum County
P.O. Box 456
Plains 79355
1-806-456-7491

Young County
P.O. Box 298
Graham 76450-0298
1-940-549-2030

Zapata County
P.O. Box 99
Zapata 78076
1-956-765-9920

Zavala County
P.O. Box 688
Crystal City 78839
1-830-374-3810

Bureaus of Vital Statistics

Texas Notaries are not permitted to make certified copies of any document that is recordable or a public record. Persons requesting "notarization," "certification" or certified copies of birth or death certificates should be referred to the appropriate public office. The following state agencies can provide certified copies of birth and death records of persons who were born or have died in the respective states, as can certain local offices not listed here:

Alabama
Center for Health Statistics
State Department of Public Health
P.O. Box 5625
Montgomery, AL 36103-5625

Alaska
Department of Health & Social Services
Bureau of Vital Statistics
P.O. Box H-02G
Juneau, AK 99811-0675

Arizona
Vital Records Section
Arizona Dept. of Health Services
P.O. Box 3887
Phoenix, AZ 85030

Arkansas
Division of Vital Records
Arkansas Department of Health
4815 West Markham Street
Little Rock, AR 72201

California
Vital Statistics Section
Department of Health Services
P.O. Box 730241
Sacramento, CA 94244-0241

Colorado
Vital Records Section
Colorado Department of Health
4300 Cherry Creek Drive South
Denver, CO 80222-1530

Connecticut
Vital Records
Department of Health Services
150 Washington Street
Hartford, CT 06106

Delaware
Office of Vital Statistics
Division of Public Health
P.O. Box 637
Dover, DE 19903

BUREAUS OF VITAL STATISTICS

District of Columbia
Vital Records Branch
425 I Street, N.W., Room 3009
Washington, DC 20001

Florida
Department of Health &
Rehabilitative Services
Office of Vital Statistics
1217 Pearl Street
P.O. Box 210
Jacksonville, FL 32231

Georgia
Georgia Dept. of Human Resources
Vital Records Unit
Room 217-H
47 Trinity Avenue, S.W.
Atlanta, GA 30334

Hawaii
Office of Health Status Monitoring
State Department of Health
P.O. Box 3378
Honolulu, HI 96801

Idaho
Vital Statistics Unit
Idaho Department of Health
& Welfare
450 West State Street
Statehouse Mail
Boise, ID 83720-9990

Illinois
Division of Vital Records
Illinois Department of Public Health
605 West Jefferson Street
Springfield, IL 62702-5097

Indiana
Vital Records Section
State Department of Health
1330 West Michigan Street
P.O. Box 1964
Indianapolis, IN 46206-1964

Iowa
Iowa Department of
Public Health
Vital Records Section
Lucas Office Building
321 East 12th Street
Des Moines, IA 50319-0075

Kansas
Office of Vital Statistics
Kansas State Department of
Health & Environment
900 Jackson Street
Topeka, KS 66612-1290

Kentucky
Office of Vital Statistics
Department for Health Services
275 East Main Street
Frankfort, KY 40621

Louisiana
Vital Records Registry
Office of Public Health
325 Loyola Avenue
New Orleans, LA 70112

Maine
Office of Vital Statistics
Maine Department of
Human Services
State House Station 11
Augusta, ME 04333-0011

Maryland
Division of Vital Records
Department of Health
and Mental Hygiene
Metro Executive Building
4201 Patterson Ave.
P.O. Box 68760
Baltimore, MD 21215-0020

Massachusetts
Registry of Vital Records
and Statistics
150 Tremont Street, Room B-3
Boston, MA 02111

Michigan
Office of the State Registrar and
Center for Health Statistics
Michigan Department of
Public Health
3423 North Logan Street
Lansing, MI 48909

Minnesota
Minnesota Department of Health
Section of Vital Statistics
717 Delaware Street, S.E.
P.O. Box 9441
Minneapolis, MN 55440

Mississippi
Vital Records
State Department of Health
2423 North State Street.
Jackson, MS 39216

Missouri
Missouri Department of Health
Bureau of Vital Records
1730 East Elm
P.O. Box 570
Jefferson City, MO 65102-0570

Montana
Bureau of Records & Statistics
State Department of Health
& Environmental Services
Helena, MT 59620

Nebraska
Bureau of Vital Statistics
State Department of Health
301 Centennial Mall South
P.O. Box 95007
Lincoln, NE 68509-5007

Nevada
Division of Health — Vital Statistics
Capitol Complex
505 East King Street, #102
Carson City, NV 89710

New Hampshire
Bureau of Vital Records
Health and Welfare Building
6 Hazen Drive
Concord, NH 03301

New Jersey
State Department of Health
Bureau of Vital Statistics
South Warren and Market
CN 370
Trenton, NJ 08625

New Mexico
Vital Statistics
New Mexico Health Services
Division
P.O. Box 26110
Santa Fe, NM 87502

New York State
Vital Records Section
State Department of Health
Empire State Plaza
Tower Building
Albany, NY 12237-0023

New York City
Division of Vital Records
New York City Department
of Health
P.O. Box 3776
New York, NY 10007

North Carolina
Department of Environment,
Health and Natural Resources
Division of Epidemiology
Vital Records Section
225 North McDowell Street
P.O. Box 29537
Raleigh, NC 27626-0537

North Dakota
Division of Vital Records
State Capitol
600 East Boulevard Avenue
Bismarck, ND 58505

Ohio
Bureau of Vital Statistics
Ohio Department of Health
P.O. Box 15098
Columbus, OH 43215-0098

BUREAUS OF VITAL STATISTICS

Oklahoma
Vital Records Section
State Department of Health
1000 Northeast 10th Street,
P.O. Box 53551
Oklahoma City, OK 73152

Oregon
Oregon Health Division
Vital Statistics Section
P.O. Box 14050
Portland, OR 97214-0050

Pennsylvania
Division of Vital Records
State Department of Health
Central Building
101 S. Mercer Street, P.O. Box 1528
New Castle, PA 16103

Rhode Island
Division of Vital Records
Rhode Island Department of Health
Room 101, Cannon Building
3 Capitol Hill
Providence, RI 02908-5097

South Carolina
Office of Vital Records & Public
Health Statistics
South Carolina Department of
Health & Environmental Control
2600 Bull Street
Columbia, SC 29201

South Dakota
State Department of Health
Center for Health Policy
and Statistics
Vital Records
523 East Capitol
Pierre, SD 57501

Tennessee
Tennessee Vital Records
Department of Health
Cordell Hull Building
Nashville, TN 37247-0350

Texas
Bureau of Vital Statistics
Texas Department of Health
1100 West 49th Street
Austin, TX 78756-3191

Utah
Bureau of Vital Records
Utah Department of Health
288 North 1460 West
P.O. Box 16700
Salt Lake City, UT 84116-0700

Vermont
Vermont Department of Health
Vital Records Section
60 Main Street, Box 70
Burlington, VT 05402

Virginia
Division of Vital Records
State Health Department
P.O. Box 1000
Richmond, VA 23208-1000

Washington
Department of Health
Center for Health Statistics
P.O. Box 9709
Olympia, WA 98507-9709

West Virginia
Vital Registration Office
Division of Health
State Capitol Complex
Building 3
Charleston, WV 25305

Wisconsin
Vital Records
1 West Wilson Street
P.O. Box 309
Madison, WI 53701

Wyoming
Vital Records Services
Hathaway Building
Cheyenne, WY 82002

American Samoa
Registrar of Vital Statistics
Vital Statistics Section
Government of American Samoa
Pago Pago, AS 96799

Guam
Office of Vital Statistics
Department of Public Health
& Social Services
Government of Guam
P.O. Box 2816
Agana, GU, M.I. 96910

Northern Mariana Islands
Superior Court
Vital Records Section
P.O. Box 307
Saipan, MP 96950

Panama Canal Zone
Panama Canal Commission
Vital Statistics Clerk
APOAA 34011

Puerto Rico
Department of Health
Demographic Registry
P.O. Box 11854
Fernández Juncos Station
San Juan, PR 00910

Virgin Islands (St. Croix)
Registrar of Vital Statistics
Charles Harwood Memorial Hospital
Christiansted, St. Croix, VI 00820

Virgin Islands (St. Thomas, St. John)
Registrar of Vital Statistics
Knud Hansen Complex
Hospital Ground
Charlotte Amalie
St. Thomas, VI 00802

Hague Convention Nations

The nations listed on the following page are parties to a treaty called the Hague Convention Abolishing the Requirement of Legalization (Authentication) for Foreign Public Documents.

Treaty Simplifies Authentication. A Notary's signature on documents that are sent to these nations may be authenticated by the Texas Secretary of State through attachment of a single certificate of capacity called an *apostille*. The *apostille* (French for "notation") is the only authentication certificate necessary. Nations not subscribing to the Hague Convention may require as many as five or six separate authenticating certificates from different governmental agencies, domestic and foreign.

How to Request an *Apostille*. To obtain an *apostille*, mail or present in person a written request (the original notarized document should *not* be forwarded) stating the Notary's name and commission expiration date with a $10 fee per document in a check payable to the "Texas Secretary of State" to:

Street Address:
Secretary of State
Notary Public Unit
1019 Brazos, #214
Austin, TX 78701

Mailing Address:
Secretary of State
Notary Public Unit
P.O. Box 13375
Austin, TX 78711-3375

An *apostille* must be specifically requested, indicating the nation to which the document will be sent.

It is *not* the Notary's responsibility to obtain an *apostille*, but rather, it is the responsibility of the party sending the document.

TEXAS NOTARY LAW PRIMER

<u>Hague Convention Nations</u>. The following nations participate in the Hague Convention:

Andorra	El Salvador
Angola[1]	Fiji
Antigua and Barbuda	Finland
Argentina[2]	France[5]
Armenia[3]	Germany
Australia	Greece
Austria	Grenada[1]
Bahamas	Guyana
Barbados	Hong Kong[6]
Belarus[3]	Hungary
Belgium	Israel
Belize	Italy
Bosnia-Herzegovina[4]	Japan
Botswana	Kiribati[1]
Brunei	Latvia
Comoros Islands[1]	Lesotho
Croatia[4]	Liberia[7]
Cyprus	Liechtenstein
Djibouti[1]	Luxembourg
Dominica[1]	Macedonia[4]

---

1. Recently independent country; has not confirmed that the Convention still applies. In accordance with Article 34(1) of the Vienna Convention on Succession of States in Respect of Treaties, the United States' view is that when a country is a party to a multilateral treaty or convention, and that country dissolves, the successor states inherit the treaty obligations of the former government.

2. Excludes recognition of extension of the Convention by the United Kingdom to the Malvinas, South Georgia, South Sandwich Islands and the Argentine Antarctic Sector.

3. Now known as the Newly Independent States. Former Union of Soviet Socialist Republics (U.S.S.R.) had signed on to the Convention, but dissolved prior to its taking effect. Only Armenia, the Belarus Republic and the Russian Federation of the former U.S.S.R. have confirmed that the Convention applies in their jurisdictions.

4. Former Yugoslavia, with its capital in the present Serbia-Montenegro, was a party to the Convention. However, only the breakaway nations of Bosnia-Herzegovina, Croatia, Macedonia and Slovenia have confirmed that the Convention still applies.

5. Including French Overseas Departments of French Guiana, French Polynesia, Guadeloupe, Martinique, New Caledonia, Reunion, St. Pierre and Miquelon, and Wallis and Futuna.

6. Retained status as Hague nation after control of Hong Kong was returned to China on July 1, 1997.

7. Convention does *not* apply between Liberia and the United States.

HAGUE CONVENTION NATIONS

Malawi	San Marino, Republic of
Malta	Seychelles
Marshall Islands	Slovenia[4]
Mauritius	Solomon Islands[1]
Mexico	South Africa
Mozambique[1]	Spain
Netherlands[8]	Suriname
Norway	Swaziland
Panama	Switzerland
Portugal[9]	Turkey
Russia[3]	Tuvalu[1]
Saint Kitts and Nevis	United Kingdom[10]
Saint Lucia	United States
Saint Vincent and	of America
the Grenadines	Vanuatu[1]

Inquiries. Persons having questions about the Hague Convention Abolishing the Requirement of Legalization for Foreign Public Documents may address their inquiries to:

> Office of American Citizen Services
> Department of State
> Washington, D.C. 20520
> 1-202-647-5225

---

1. Recently independent country; has not confirmed that the Convention still applies. In accordance with Article 34(1) of the Vienna Convention on Succession of States in Respect of Treaties, the United States' view is that when a country is a party to a multilateral treaty or convention, and that country dissolves, the successor states inherit the treaty obligations of the former government.

3. Now known as the Newly Independent States. Former Union of Soviet Socialist Republics (U.S.S.R.) had signed on to the Convention, but dissolved prior to its taking effect. Only Armenia, the Belarus Republic and the Russian Federation of the former U.S.S.R. have confirmed that the Convention applies in their jurisdictions.

4. Former Yugoslavia, with its capital in the present Serbia-Montenegro, was a party to the Convention. However, only the breakaway nations of Bosnia-Herzegovina, Croatia, Macedonia and Slovenia have confirmed that the Convention still applies.

8. Extended to Aruba, Curacao and Netherlands Antilles.

9. Extended to Macao and all overseas territories.

10. United Kingdom of Great Britain and Northern Ireland is extended to Anguilla, Bermuda, British Antarctica Territory, British Virgin Islands, Cayman Islands, Falkland Islands, Gibraltar, Guernsey, Isle of Man, Jersey, Montserrat, Saint Georgia and the South Sandwich Islands, Saint Helena, Tonga, Turks and Caicos Islands, and Zimbabwe.

About the Publisher

Since 1957, The National Notary Association, a nonprofit educational organization, has served the nation's Notaries Public — today numbering nearly four and a half million — with a wide variety of instructional programs and services.

As the country's clearinghouse for information on notarial laws, customs and practices, the NNA educates Notaries through publications, seminars, annual conferences and a *Notary Information Service* that offers immediate answers to specific questions about notarization.

The Association is perhaps most widely known as the preeminent publisher of information for and about Notaries. NNA works include:

- *The National Notary*, a magazine for National Notary Association members featuring how-to articles with practical tips on notarizing.

- *Notary Bulletin*, keeping NNA members up to date on developments affecting Notaries, especially new state laws and regulations.

- *Notary Basics Made Easy*, a first-of-its-kind video instruction program that simplifies Notary practices and procedures.

- *Notary Home Study Course*, a work-at-your-own-speed course covering every facet of notarization.

- *Sorry, No Can Do!* and *Sorry, No Can Do! 2*, two volumes that help Notaries explain to customers why some requests for notarizations are improper and cannot be accommodated.

- *Notary Seal & Certificate Verification Manual*, invaluable for any person relying on the authenticity and correctness of legal documents created or filed in the United States.

- *Notary Public Practices & Glossary*, widely hailed as the Notary's bible, a definitive reference book on notarial procedures.

- *Notary Law Primers*, explaining particular states' notarial statutes in easy-to-understand language.

- The *Model Notary Act*, prototype legislation conceived in 1973 and updated in 1984 by an NNA-recruited panel of secretaries of state, legislators and attorneys, and regularly used by state legislatures in revising their notarial laws.

- *Notary Law & Practice: Cases & Materials*, the definitive and one-of-a-kind text for teaching Notary law to students in law schools and to attorneys in Minimum Continuing Legal Education (MCLE) seminars, discussing every major judicial decision affecting the Notary's duties.

- Public-service pamphlets informing the general public about the function of a Notary, including *What Is A Notary Public?*, printed in both English and Spanish.

In addition, the National Notary Association provides Notaries with the highest quality professional supplies, including official seals and stamps, embossers, record-keeping journals, affidavit stamps, thumbprinting devices and notarial certificates.

Though dedicated primarily to educating and assisting Notaries, the National Notary Association devotes part of its resources to helping lawmakers draft effective notarial statutes and to informing the public about the Notary's vital role in modern society. ■

Index

A

Acknowledgment 21, **22–26**, 77, 88, 92–96
   Acknowledge signature 23
   Certificates for . . **23–25**, 79–81, 94–96
   Common act. 22
   Date 77
   Defined 79
   Fees **49**, 76, 90
   Identification of signer. 23, 25, **40–41**, 94
   Journal requirement. 97–98
   Out-of-country 26
   Out-of-state. 26
   Purpose **22–23**, 93
   Requirements. **22–23**, 93
   Terminology 25
   Who may take **25–26**, 92–93
   Witnessing signature . . . 10–11, 23, **25**
Address, change of **20**, 74, 90
Advertising, foreign-language . . .**57–58**, 62, 74, 89
Advice (see "Law, unauthorized practice of") 16, **53–54**, 58, 60, 74, 78, 89
Affidavit **30–31**, 79
   Affirmation for **31**, 33
   Certificate for 31, **32**
   Definition **30**, 79
   Purpose **30**, 79
   Oath for **31**, 33
Affirmation 21, **33–34**, 79, 82
   Affidavit, for 31, **33**
   Ceremony. 34

Certificate for *82*
Credible identifying witnesses, for 33–34, **42**
Defined *79*
Deposition, for 31, **33**
Fees **50**, *76, 90*
Gestures 34
Jurat, for 32–33
Power to administer 33
Proof of acknowledgment by handwriting, for 36
Proof of acknowledgment by subscribing witness, for. 38
Purpose **33**, *79*
Response required 34
Subscribing witness, for **34**, 38
Wording 33–34
Apostilles **56–57**, *113–115*
Authentication 56–57
   Apostilles **56–57**, *113–115*
   Fees 56–57
   Hague Convention Abolishing the Requirement of Legalization for Foreign Public Documents. 56–57, **113–115**
   Hague Convention nations . . . *114–115*
   Out of state 56
   Out of country 56
   Procedure 56–57
Authenticity, certificate of (see "Authentication") 56
Authority, certificate of (see "Authentication") 56

Page numbers listed in **bold** indicate where the most complete information on a subject can be found. *Italics* indicate the pages where the statutes pertaining to a subject are located.

118

INDEX

Authority of Notary *88–89*

B

Beneficial interest (see "Disqualifying interest") 8, 10, 37, 42, **51–52**, *76–77*
Birth certificate, certified copy of 10, 27, *77–78*
   Blank spaces in document **13**,
Bond, Notary 4, **18–19**, *72, 87*
   Filing 4, **19**, *87*
   Liability of Notary and surety **19**, *72–73*
   Protects public 19
   Requirement **18–19**, *72, 87*
Bureaus of Vital Statistics 108–112

C

Capacity, certificate of (see "Authentication") 56
Capacity of signer **40–41**, 45
Certificates, notarial 6, 14–15, **46–48**, *79–84, 94–97*
   Acknowledgment, for **23–25**, *80–81, 94–96*
   Affidavit, for 31, **32**
   Affirmation, for *82*
   Alteration of authorized certificates **25**, *77, 94*
   Certified copy, for **27–28**, *84*
   Certified copy of notarial record, for **28–29**, 46
   Choosing 14–15, 16, **53**, *78*
   Copy certification by document custodian, for 29
   Contents 46–47
   Deposition, for **30–31**, *83*
   Jurat **32**, *81*
   Loose certificates 15–16, **47–48**
   Modification of authorized certificates **25**, *77, 94*
   Oath, for *82*
   Pre-sign or seal 48
   Proof of acknowledgment by handwriting, for 35–36
   Proof of acknowledgment by subscribing witness, for **37–38**, *96–97*
   Protest, for **39–40**, *83–84*
   Requirement 46–47
   Seal of Notary 47
   Signature by mark, for 54
   Signature of Notary 47
   Statement of particulars 47
   Testimonium clause 47

Venue 46
Verification, for *81–82*
Certificate of authentication (see "Authentication") 56
Certificate of authority (see "Authentication") 56
Certificate of capacity (see "Authentication") 56
Certificate of official character (see "Authentication") 56
Certificate of prothonotary (see "Authentication") 56
Certified copies 10, 21, **26–28**, *88*
   Birth certificate, of 10, **27**, *77–78*
   Certificate for **27–28**, *84*
   County clerk, by **27**, *88*
   Death certificate, of. . . . 10, **27**, *77–78*
   Fees **49**, *90*
   Precautions 27
   Procedure **26–27**, *77–78*
   Purpose 26
   Recordable documents, of **27**, *61, 77–78*
   Vital records, of 10, **27**
Certified copy of notarial record . . **28–29**, *73, 88*
   Certificate for **28–29**, 46
   Fees 49, *76, 90*
   Procedure 28
   Written request 28
Civil Practices and Remedies Code:
   Section 121.001 . . . . 21, 25, 26, 59, *92*
   Section 121.002 . . . . 52, *93*
   Section 121.003 . . . . 36, 38, *93*
   Section 121.004 . . . . *93*
   Section 121.005 . . . . 22, 25, 40, 41, 42, *94*
   Section 121.006 . . . . 22, 25, 41, *94*
   Section 121.007 . . . . 23, *94*
   Section 121.008 . . . . 23, *95*
   Section 121.009 . . . . 37, *96*
   Section 121.010 . . . . 37, *96*
   Section 121.011 . . . . 34, 35, 54, *97*
   Section 121.012 . . . . 43, *98*
   Section 121.013 . . . . 36, 38, *98*
   Section 121.014 . . . . 52, 60, 63, *98*
Commission, Notary 17–21
   Address, change of **20**, *74, 90*
   Application 3–4, **17–18**, *61–63, 86–87*
   Appointment *85–86*
   Bond 4, **18–19**, *72, 87*
   Denial of **61–63**, *75, 86–87*
   Education materials *71–84*
   Fees **18**, *86*
   Jurisdiction **19**, *77, 85*

119

Military-officers. 26, **59**, *92–93*
Name, change of **20–21**, *77*
Oath for 4, **19**, *72*, 87
Qualifications. 3, **17–18**, *86*
Reappointment 3, 4, **18**, 87
Rejection of application 18, *75*
Renewal 3, 4, **18**, 87
Resignation **20**, *89–90*
Revocation **61–63**, *73*,
                      75, 86–87, 89
Suspension **61–63**, *73*,
                      75, 86–87, 89
Term **20**, *85*
Competence, determining 12–13
Conformed copy 9
Copy certification by document
  custodian 29
  Certificate 29
  Jurat for 29
  Purpose 29
Copy certification by Notary (see
  "Certified copies") 10, 21, **26–28**
County Clerks' offices 100–107
Credible identifying witness 8, 40,
                                41–42
  Affirmation for 33–34, **42**
  Identification of. 42
  Journal entry 42
  Oath for. 33–34, **42**
  Purpose 41
  Qualifications 41–42
  Signature in journal 42
  Subscribing witness confusion 42
Customers, restricting services to 9

D

Date of document **14**, *77*
Death certificate, certified copy of . . .10
Deposition 21, **30–31**, *88*
  Affirmation for **31**, 33
  Certificate for **30–31**, *83*
  Definition 30
  Fees **50**, *76, 90*
  Oath for **31**, 33
  Purpose 30
Disabled person, signing for .**54–55**, *89*
Disqualifying interest 11, **51–52**, *93*
  Beneficial interest 51–52
  Corporate officers **52**, *93*
  Employees 52
  Financial interest 51–52

Relatives 11, **52**, *76–77*
Shareholders. **52**, *93*
Documents:
  Alter or change 77
  Blank spaces **13**, 16, 53
  Date, checking **14**, 77
  Incomplete **13**, 16, 53
  Preparation of 16, **53**, *78*
  Scan for information 14
  Selection of 16, **53**, *78*
Duties *72–73, 88–89*

E

Education Materials, Notary
  Public *71–84*
Embosser, Notary seal 5, **48**, *87–88*
Equipment 5–6
Errors and omissions insurance 6
Exam, trial *65–70*
Ex Officio Notary 20

F

Family members, notarizing for (see
  "Disqualifying interest") . . .11, **51–52**,
                                    76–77
Fees **49–51**, *76, 90*
  Acknowledgments, for **49**, *76, 90*
  Affirmations, for **50**, *76, 90*
  Certified copy, for 49
  Copy of notarial record, for 45,
                            49–50, *76, 90*
  Depositions, for. **50**, *76, 90*
  Fee book 44–45, **51**,
                              75, 91–92
  Itemize **51**, *75, 91–92*
  Journal entry 45, **49–50**
  Jurats, for **50**, *76, 90*
  Maximum **49–51**, *76, 90*
  Oaths, for **50**, *76, 90*
  Option not to charge 50
  Other notarial acts **50**, *76, 90*
  Overcharging **50–51**, 61,
                            62, *78, 92*
  Posting 4, **51**, *75, 92*
  Proofs of acknowledgment by
    handwriting, for **50**, *76, 90*
  Proofs of acknowledgment by
    subscribing witness, for . . **50**, *76, 90*
  Protests, for. **50**, *76, 90*
  Receipt for **51**, *92*
  Record of 44–45, **51**, *75, 91–92*

Page numbers listed in **bold** indicate where the most complete information on a subject can be found. *Italics* indicate the pages where the statutes pertaining to a subject are located.

INDEX

Travel. 50
Financial interest (see
　"Disqualifying interest") 51–52
Fines (see "Misconduct") 60–64
Foreign languages 9–10, **57–58**
　Advertising **57**, 62, 74, 89
　Documents. 9–10, **57–58**
　Signers 10, **58**
　Translation of "Notary Public" into
　　Spanish **61**, 74, 78, 89
Flags (see "Authentication") 56

G

Government Code:
　Section 406.001 85
　Section 406.002. . . . . 20, 85
　Section 406.003. . . . . 19, 85
　Section 406.004. . . . . 17, 85
　Section 406.005. . . . . 19, 85
　Section 406.006. . . . . 18, 86
　Section 406.007. . . . . 18, 86
　Section 406.008. . . . . 71, 86
　Section 406.009. . . . . . . 18, 22, 51, 61,
　　　　　　　　　　62, 63, 64, 75, 86
　Section 406.010 . . . . 18, 19, 87
　Section 406.011. . . . . 18, 87
　Section 406.012 87
　Section 406.013. . . . . 48, 87
　Section 406.014. . . . . . . 26, 28, 42, 43,
　　　　　　　　　　　44, 45, 73, 88
　Section 406.015. . . . . 27, 88
　Section 406.016. . . . . . . 21, 22, 26, 27,
　　　　　　　　　　30, 33, 39, 53,
　　　　　　　　　　58, 60, 61, 77, 88
　Section 406.0165 . . . . 54, 89
　Section 406.017 . . . . 18, 57, 61,
　　　　　　　　　　　62, 63, 74, 89
　Section 406.018 . . . . 63, 89
　Section 406.019 . . . . 20, 74, 90
　Section 406.020 . . . . 20, 63, 90
　Section 406.021 . . . . 20, 63, 90
　Section 406.022. . . . . . . 20, 46, 62, 90
　Section 406.023. 90
　Section 406.024. . . . . . . 45, 49, 51, 61,
　　　　　　　　　　　62, 76, 77, 90
　Section 406.051. 91
　Section 406.052. 91
　Section 406.053. 91
　Section 406.054. 91
　Section 406.055. 91
　Section 603.001. 91
　Section 603.006. . . . . . . 45, 51, 75, 91
　Section 603.007 . . . . 51, 75, 92
　Section 603.008 . . . . 51, 75, 92
　Section 603.010. . . . . . . 51, 61, 62, 92

H

Hague Convention Abolishing
　the Requirement of Legalization for
　Foreign Public
　Documents 56–57, **113–115**

I

Identification 12, **40–43**, 94
　Acknowledgment, for 22–23, 25,
　　　　　　　　　　　　　　40, 94
　Capacity of signer. **40–41**, 45
　Credible identifying witness 8, 40,
　　　　　　　　　　　　　　41–42
　Documents **42–43**, 78
　Journal entry. 44
　Minors, of 55–56
　Other notarial acts, for. . 10–11, 32, **40**
　Personal knowledge. 40, **41**
　Satisfactory evidence 40
　Subscribing witness, for **37**, 96
Identification documents . . . **42–43**, 78
　Acceptable **42–43**, 78
　Fraudulent 43
　Multiple 43
　Unacceptable **43**, 78
Immigration 58
　Advice 58
　Documents. 58
　Naturalization certificates **58**, 61
Impartiality (see "Disqualifying
　interest") 11, **51–52**, 93
Incomplete documents **13**, 16, 53
Insurance, errors and omissions 6
Interpreters for proofs of
　acknowledgment 38

J

Journal of notarial acts 4, 5–6, 14,
　　　　　　　　　　　　　　43–46, 73,
　　　　　　　　　　　　　　88, 97–98
　Copies of records . . **28–29**, 45–46, 73
　County Clerk exemption 43–44
　Credible identifying witness,
　　entry for 42
　Disposition of **46**, 62
　Entries, additional 45
　Entries required 5–6, 14, **43–46**,
　　　　　　　　　　　　　73, 88, 97–98
　Inspection of **45**, 87, 97–98
　Requirement. **43**, 73, 87, 97–98
　Signature by mark, entry for 54
　Surrender of 46
　Thumbprint. 6, 45
Jurat 21, **32–33**, 79
　Affirmation for 32–33

121

TEXAS NOTARY LAW PRIMER

Certificate for **32**, *81*
Fees 50
Oath for 32–33
Purpose **32**, *79*
Identification 10–11, **32**
Signature 10–11, **32**
Stamp 6
Jurisdiction **19**, *77, 85*

L

Law, unauthorized practice of . . . **53–54**,
  60, *74, 78, 89*
 Advice 16, **54**, 58,
  60, *78, 89*
 Assistance **53**, 60, *89*
 Blanks in document 13, 16, **53**
 Exceptions 53–54
 Preparation of document 16, **53**,
  60, *78*
 Selection of document 16, **53**, *78*
 Selection of notarization 14–15,
  16, **53**, *78*
Laws pertaining to notarization . . *84–98*
Legalization
 (see "Authentication") 56–57
Liability of Notary . . . **63–64**, *72–73, 98*
Locus sigilli 15, 47, **49**
Loose certificates 15–16, **47–48**
L.S. 15, 47, **49**

M

Mark, signature by 54
 Certificate for 54
 Procedures 54
 Witnesses 54
Marriages 22
Military-officer notarizations 26, **59**,
  92–93
Minors, notarizing for 55–56
 Identification 55–56
 Procedure 55
 Signature 55
Misconduct **60–64**, *75, 78–79,
  86–87, 89–90*
 Advertising, improper
  foreign-language 57, **62**, *89*
 Appeal of penalty **64**, *75*
 Application misstatement 62
 Certify copy of recordable
  document 27, 61, *77–78*
 Civil liability **63–64**, *72–73, 98*

Denial of appointment . **61–63**, *86–87*
Failure of duty 63, *89–90*
Felony conviction 62
Fines 60–64
Hearing, right to **64**, *75*
Issue identification 22, **61**,
  78–79, 88–89
Law, unauthorized practice of . **53–54**,
  60, *74, 78, 89*
Liability **63–64**, *72–73, 98*
Marriages 22
Naturalization certificate copies or
 notarizations, improper **58**, 61
Neglect of duty **63**, *89–90*
Notarize own signature . 22, **61**, *78–79*
Notarize under another name **61**,
  78–79
Notary law violation 62, *86–87*
Notice, right to **64**, *75*
Overcharging . . . **50–51**, 61, 62, *78, 92*
Personal appearance, failure
 to require **61**, 63, *78–79*
Recordable document, certify
 copy of 27, **61**, *77–78*
Rejection of application . . . 18, *86–87*
Residency, failure to
 maintain **63**, *90*
Resignation **20**, *90*
Revocation of commission **60–64**,
  75, 86–87
Seal, failure to affix **60**, *78–79*
Signature, notarize own 22, **61**,
  78–79
Spanish translation of
 "Notary Public" **61**, *74, 78, 89*
Suspension of commission **60–64**,
  75, 86–87
Telephone notarizations . . . **22**, 63, *77*
Translation of "Notary Public" into
 Spanish **61**, *74, 78, 89*

N

Name, change of **20–21**, *77*
National Notary Association 116–117
Naturalization certificates **58**, 61
Notarial acts 21–40
 Acknowledgment 21, **22–26**,
  77, 88, 92–96
 Affidavit **30–31**, *79*
 Affirmation 21, **33–34**, *79, 82*
 Authorized acts 21–22, *88–89*

Page numbers listed in **bold** indicate where the most complete information on a subject can be found. *Italics* indicate the pages where the statutes pertaining to a subject are located.

122

INDEX

Certified copies.... 10, 21, **26–28**, 88
Certified copies of notarial record **28–29**, 73, 88
Choosing 14–15, 16, **53**, 78
Copy certification by document custodian. 29
Deposition.......... 21, **30–31**, 88
Jurat 21, **32–33**, 79
Oath......... 21, **33–34**, 79, 88–89
Proof of acknowledgment by handwriting 21, **34–36**, 97
Proof of acknowledgment by subscribing witness..... 21, **36–38**, 88–89, 96
Proof of execution (see "Proof of acknowledgment by subscribing witness") 21, **36–38**, 88–89, 96
Protest 22, **38–40**, 79, 83–84, 88–89
Unauthorized acts........ 22, 78–79
Notarial certificates (see "Certificates, notarial") 6, 14–15, **46–48**, 79–84, 94–97
Notarial records (see "Journal of notarial acts") 4, 5–6, 14, 28–29, **43–46**, 73, 88, 97–98
Notarial seal (see "Seal, notarial") ...4, 5, 15, **48–49**, 73–74, 87–88
Notary Public Education Materials 71–84
Notary seal (see "Seal, notarial") ...4, 5, 15, **48–49**, 73–74, 87–88

O

Oath .... .21, **33–34**, 79, 88–89
Affidavit, for 31, **33**
Ceremony................... 34
Certificate for 82
Credible identifying witnesses, for 33–34, **42**
Deposition, for 31, **33**
Fees................. **50**, 76, 90
Gestures.................... 34
Jurat, for 32–33
Power to administer 33, 88–89
Proof of acknowledgment by handwriting, for 36
Proof of acknowledgment by subscribing witness, for........ 38
Purpose **33**, 79
Response required............. 34
Subscribing witness, for 38
Wording 33–34
Oath of office, Notary's 4, **19**, 85–86, 87
Filing............ 4, **19**, 85–86, 87
Requirement **19**, 85–86, 87

P

Penalties (see "Misconduct") **60–64**, 75, 78–79, 86–87, 89–90
Personal appearance **12**, 22–23, 61, 77, 78
Personal knowledge of identity .... .40, **41**, 94
Photocopies 9
Photographs, notarizing 8
Practices and procedures 40–60
Proof of acknowledgment by handwriting .... .21, **34–36**, 97
Affirmation for 36
Certificate for............... 35–36
Deposition or affidavit requirement.............. **35**, 97
Fees................. **50**, 76, 90
In lieu of acknowledgment.... 35, 97
Oath for 36
Purpose 34
Requirements **35**, 97
Subpoena of witness... 36, 38, **93**, 98
Witnesses................ 35, 97
Proof of acknowledgment by subscribing witness 21–22, **36–38**, 88–89, 92–93, 96–97
Affirmation for subscribing witness 34, **38**
Authority to perform... 88–89, 92–93
Certificate for **37–38**, 96–97
Fees................. **50**, 76, 90
Identity of subscribing witness . **37**, 96
In lieu of acknowledgment 36–37
Interpreters, employment of... **38**, 93
Journal entry 38, 97–98
Oath for subscribing witness 34, **38**
Subpoena of witness... 36, **38**, 93, 98
Subscribing witness 37
Purpose **36**, 96
Signature of subscribing witness **37**, 96
Proof of execution (see "Proof of acknowledgment") 21–22, **36–38**
Protest .... .22, **38–40**, 79, 83–84, 88–89
Antiquated act................ 39
Certificate for........ **39–40**, 83–84
Fees................. **50**, 76, 90
Purpose **38–39**, 79
Special knowledge required 39

123

Prothonotary, certificate of (see
"Authentication") 56

Q
Qualifications 3, **17–18**, *86*

R
Reasonable care 12–16, **52–53**
Records (see "Journal of
notarial acts") 4, 5–6, 14,
43–46, 73, *88, 97–98*
Refusal of services 52
Resignation of commission . . .**20**, *89–90*
Restricting services 9
Revocation of commission (see
"Misconduct") **60–64**, 75,
78–79, 86–87, 89–90

S
Satisfactory evidence of identity 40
Scilicet 46
SCT. 46
Seal, notarial 4, 5, 15, **48–49**,
73–74, 87–88
Affixing. **15**, 87–88
Embosser 5, **48**, 87–88
Failure to affix **60**, 78–79
Format 5, **48**, 73–74, 87–88
Information required **48–49**,
73–74, 87–88
Inking seal 5, **48**, 87–88
L.S. 15, 47, **49**
No room for 8–9
Placement of. 49
Requirement. 47, **48**,
73–74, 87–88
Smearing. 8–9, **48**
Secretary of State office 3, **99**
Self-notarization 22, **61**, 78–79
Signature
Certificate, on 47
Checking 13
In presence of Notary 10
Journal 44
Minor, of 55
Mark, signature by 54
Notarizing one's own 22,
61, 78–79
Notary's 15, **47**
Signature by mark 54
Certificate for 54

Procedures 54
Witnesses .54
SS. 46
Statement of particulars
(see "Certificate") 47
Statutes pertaining to
notarization *84–98*
Subpoena of witness 36, 38, *93, 98*
Subscribing witness (see "Proof of
execution by subscribing
witness") 37
Supplies .5–6
Surety .18–19
Suspension of commission (see
"Misconduct") **60–64**, 75, 78–79,
86–87, 89–90

T
Telephone notarizations **22**, 63, 77
Term of office, Notary's **20**, *85*
Testimonium clause
(see "Certificate") 47
Thumbprint, journal 6, 45
Device. 6
Tools, Notary 5–6

U
U.S. Code:
10 U.S.C. Sec. 936 59
10 U.S.C. Sec. 1044a 59
18 U.S.C. Sec. 137 . . . . 58, 61
U.S. Penal Code:
Section 75 . . . . 58, 61

V
Venue (see "Certificate") 46
Stamp 6
Verification **32**, *79, 81–82*
Vital records, notarizing . .10, **27**, *77–78*
Vital Statistics, Bureaus of *108–112*

W
Weddings (see "Marriages") 22
Willingness, determining 12–13
Wills 7–8, **60**
Advice or assistance. 60
Certificate wording required 60
Living wills. 60
Witness jurats (see "Proof of
acknowledgment by subscribing
witness") 21–22, **36–38**, *96–97*

Page numbers listed in **bold** indicate where the most complete information on a subject can be found. *Italics* indicate the pages where the statutes pertaining to a subject are located.

Because you can't know everything...

You Should Belong to the National Notary Association

It doesn't matter whether you're a long-time Notary, or a newcomer. Whether you notarize dozens of documents each week, or a few a month.

As a Notary, you should belong to the National Notary Association.

We're a professional association with over 150,000 members from every state and U.S. jurisdiction. And we've devoted our efforts to your needs and concerns for over four decades.

There are many reasons to be a part of the NNA. Among them:

- *The National Notary* magazine... A bimonthly magazine packed with enlightening articles, helpful how-to features, handy tips and useful advice.

- The *Notary Bulletin* newspaper... This bimonthly newspaper keeps you up-to-date on law and procedure changes in your state, and helps you comply with new laws.

- Discount Notary Supplies... You'll save up to 40% on the supplies you need, including Notary journals, official seals, certificates and more.

With these services and so much more, we're here for you when you need us. You should belong to the National Notary Association.

National Notary Association
9350 De Soto Ave., P.O. Box 2402
Chatsworth, CA 91313-2402
Telephone: 1-800-US NOTARY (1-800-876-6827)
Fax: 1-800-833-1211
www.nationalnotary.org

Other Resources from the National Notary Association

'Notary Law & Practice: Cases & Materials'
...The definitive legal text on notarization. Authored by five noted law school professors, *Notary Law & Practice* presents scores of notarization-related court decisions and details how these cases affect you today. You get extensive judicial opinions and commentary about notarizations and related frauds. Hardcover, 6¼" x 9¼", 629 pages.

No. 5100............................$49.95 NNA members / $68.00 non-NNA members

'Notary Home Study Course'
...Step-by-step, illustrated instructions for all the notarial acts you'll likely perform. You'll learn how to complete the many certificates you'll see, notarize unusual documents, avoid common pitfalls, and prevent personal liability. Learn time-saving shortcuts you can take...and can't take. The *Notary Home Study Course* will make your duties as a Notary much, much easier! Softcover, 8¼" x 10¾", 448 pages.

No. 5001............................$34.95 NNA members / $48.00 non-NNA members

'Notary Seal & Certificate Verification Manual'
...Essential for legal and business professionals and government officials who receive or send documents out-of-state. At a glance, the *Notary Seal & Certificate Verification Manual* gives you detailed notarization rules and procedures for all 50 states, the District of Columbia, and five U.S. jurisdictions. Softcover, 8¼" x 10¾", 423 pages.

No. 5143............................$44.95 NNA members / $79.00 non-NNA members

'Notary Basics Made Easy' Video Instruction Program
...Makes reviewing Notary basics as easy as watching TV. From checking signer's identification to affixing your signature and seal, *Notary Basics Made Easy* gives you the know-how you need to begin or enhance your career as a Notary. Complete set includes three VHS video tapes and a handy 16-page Program Guide. Approximate running time: 50 minutes.

No. 5009............................$29.95 NNA members / $50.00 non-NNA members

'State Notary Law Primers'
...Detailed instructions on Notary laws and regulations in the following states:

Arizona ....No. 5130	Missouri ....No. 5122	Oregon ....No. 5128
California........No. 5120	Nevada ....No. 5134	Texas ....No. 5123
Florida ....No. 5121	New Jersey ......No. 5131	Utah..............No. 5127
Hawaii............No. 5132	New York ....No. 5125	Washington ....No. 5124
Michigan ....No. 5135	No. Carolina ....No. 5129	*(More states in production.)*

Softcover, 124 to 128 pages, 5¼" x 8⅜"......$12.95 NNA members / $16.00 non-NNA members

---

National Notary Association
To order, use the form on the back of the opposite page, or call 1-800-876-6827.

'101 Useful Notary Tips'
...Tips on every subject, from acknowledgments and apostilles...to jurats and journals...to seals and signatures make this a perfect, quick reference guide. Softcover, 5½" x 8¼", 46 pages.

No. 5119 .... $8.95 NNA members / $14.00 non-NNA members

'12 Steps to a Flawless Notarization'
...Explains how to perform a problem-free notarization, including screening identification, scanning a document and filling out notarial wording. Softcover, 5¼" x 8¼", 48 pages.

No. 5144 .... $8.95 NNA members / $14.00 non-NNA members

'ID Checking Guide'
...Pictures and specifications for each state's driver's license, descriptions of non-driver, military and immigration IDs, and credit cards. Drivers License Guide Co., softcover, 6" x 9", 96 pages.

No. 5599.......................... $17.95 NNA members / $20.00 non-NNA members

'How to Fingerprint'
...Shows you all the steps for taking clear, useable fingerprints for employment, for a special office or for identification of minors. Softcover, 5¼" x 8¼", 110 pages.

No. 5102.......................... $12.95 NNA members / $18.00 non-NNA members

'How to Take a Notary Journal Thumbprint'
...Explains how a journal thumbprint protects the Notary, document signers and the public. Provides details on how to obtain clear, useable prints. Softcover, 5¼" x 8¼", 64 pages.

No. 5140 .... $8.95 NNA members / $14.00 non-NNA members

'Notary Public Practices & Glossary'
...Covers every important facet of the Notary Public office and provides definitive explanations of notarial procedures. Hardcover, 5½" x 8¾", 176 pages.

No. 5110.......................... $15.95 NNA members / $22.00 non-NNA members

'Preparing for the California Notary Public Exam'
...Helps you get ready for and pass the exam by explaining California's stringent Notary laws and focusing on what is important for the exam. Softcover, 5¼" x 8¼", 88 pages.

No. 2000.......................... $12.95 NNA members / $18.00 non-NNA members

'Sorry, No Can Do!' & 'Sorry, No Can Do! 2'
...Easy-to-understand responses to the most common requests for improper notarizations. When asked to preform an improper act, you can show your signer the relevant page and they'll see why you have to turn down the request. Hardcover, 5¼" x 8¼", spiral bound to lay flat.

2 Volume Set, No. 5386 .... $21.95 NNA members / $30.00 non-NNA members

---

National Notary Association
To order, use the form on the back of this page, or call 1-800-876-6827.

Order Form

Membership Information

☐ **YES! I want to receive the benefits of membership in the National Notary Association!** Please enroll me as a member for the following term:

☐ 1 Year $34
☐ 2 Years $59 – save $9.00!
☐ 3 Years $79 – save $23.00!
☐ 4 Years $99 – save $37.00!
☐ 5 Years – $119 save $51.00!

Please include your membership dues in total below. There is no tax or shipping charge on your NNA membership.

Item #	Quantity	Description	Price	TOTAL

SHIPPING

Subtotal	Shipping
UNDER $15	$3.85
$15.01 – $35.00	$4.85
$35.01 – $65.00	$5.85
$65.01 – $95.00	$6.85
$95.01+	$7.85

Subtotal

Add state and local taxes on subtotal for:
AZ, CA, FL, MI, MO, NV, NJ, NY, TX & WA

Add Shipping

Add Membership Dues

TOTAL Enclosed

Shipping/Payment Information

Name

Organization

Address ☐ Business ☐ Home

City

State   Zip

Daytime Phone

Fax

E-Mail Address

NNA Member Number (Required for member prices)

☐ Check Enclosed — Payable to: National Notary Association

☐ Visa ☐ MasterCard ☐ American Express ☐ Discover

Card Number

Card Expires

Signature

Sorry, but we cannot accept purchase orders to bill on account.

Four Easy Ways to Order:

By Phone: 1-800-876-6827
(1-800-US NOTARY) with credit card order

By FAX: 1-800-833-1211
24 hours with credit card order

By Mail: NNA Notary Supplies Division
9350 De Soto Ave., P.O. Box 2402
Chatsworth, CA 91313-2402

By Internet: www.nationalnotary.org
24 hours with credit card order

National Notary Association

Office use only.

Service Code
A15745